UP'

AND RUNNING

IN 30 DAYS

A Proven Plan for Financial
Success in Real Estate

Carla Cross

Dearborn™
Real Estate Education

While a great deal of care has been taken to provide accurate and current information, the ideas, suggestions, general principles and conclusions presented in this text are subject to local, state, and federal laws and regulations, court cases, and any revisions of the same. The reader is thus urged to consult legal counsel regarding any points of law—this publication should not be used as a substitute for competent legal advice.

Vice President: Roy Lipner
Publisher: Evan Butterfield
Development Editor: Anne Huston
Senior Managing Editor: Ronald J. Liszkowski
Copy Editor: Genevieve Gwynne
Typesetting: Janet Schroeder
Art and Design Manager: Lucy Jenkins

Published by Dearborn™ Real Estate Education,
a division of Dearborn Financial Publishing, Inc.®,
30 South Wacker Drive
Chicago, IL 60606-7481
(312) 836-4400
http://www.dearbornRE.com

Library of Congress Cataloging-in-Publication Data

Cross, Carla.
  Up and running in 30 days: a proven plan for financial success in real estate / by Carla
Cross—2nd ed.
    p.cm.
  Includes bibliographical references and index.
  ISBN 0-7931-4485-X
    1. Real estate agents—United States 2. Real estate business—United States—Marketing.
  I. Title: Up and running in thirty days. II. Title

HD278.C76 2001
333.33'068'8—dc21

2001017382

DEDICATION

Up and Running in 30 Days has been inspired by people from two worlds, at once disparate yet exhibiting many more similarities than differences—the worlds of musical performance and real estate sales.

At four I sat down at the piano to pick out the melody and chords to popular songs. That early love of music led to years of performing on piano and flute in front of thousands of people. It also introduced me to the performance concepts that assure mastery of skills. For those indelible lessons in performance this book is dedicated to two influential teachers—Stacy Green, University of Oregon piano instructor, and Del Chinburg, my flute teacher in grade and high school. You'll find in this book references to "perfect practice makes perfect," "precision in following the process," and "improvising after you know the tune." These aphorisms aren't mine. They were taught to me by these master performer-teachers, and I learned them by doing them—the only way to learn.

I stumbled into the world of real estate sales by chance, simply to help my husband. Although I didn't realize it at the time, the musical performance skills I had perfected as a concert artist were exactly what I needed to hone and master the skills of real estate sales. For believing in my abilities and answering my innumerable questions, I acknowledge my first real estate "boss," Robert Grace, who taught me to "just do it." "Go meet people" was his mantra—so, student that I am, I did just that.

Perfect practice makes perfect. We learn by doing. Mastering something takes dedication, tenacity, and determination over time. These are the lessons my mentors taught me, and these are the lessons in this book. Thank you for allowing me to pass the lessons of my teachers and mentors on to you.

—Carla Cross

CONTENTS

Preface   ix

Introduction   xi

SECTION 1:   Heads Up: New Trends That Will Affect How You Do Business 1

Trend Number One: Evolving Company Structures   2
Trend Number Two: Relationship Marketing   4
Trend Number Three: Systematization   5
Trend Number Four: Technology   5
Trend Number Five: Training   6
Trend Number Six: Coaching   9
Trend Number Seven: Teaming   10

SECTION 2:   The Five Principles of a High-Producing Business   11

Principle One: Start the Business Cycle   12
Principle Two: Stay on the Business Path   13
Principle Three: Prioritize Your Activities   13
Principle Four: Prospect Like the Pros   16
Principle Five: Work the Numbers   22
Up and Running Puts All the Business Principles Together   25
All Your Self-Management Tools   30

SECTION 3:   Four Weeks to Becoming a Successful Agent   31

Managing Your Program   32
Managing Your Attitude   34
The Manager's Role   40
Up and Running: An Overview of Your Four Weeks   43

SECTION 4:   Week One   59

Objectives   60
Weekly Activity Plan   61
Business Development   61
Business Support   70
Preparation for Reactive Prospective Activities   73
Final Thoughts for Week One   73

SECTION 5:   Week Two   77

Objectives   78
Weekly Activity Plan   78
Business Development   86
Business Support   87
Final Thoughts for Week Two   89

SECTION 6:   Week Three   93

Objectives   94
Weekly Activity Plan   94
Business Development   104
Business Support   104
Final Thoughts for Week Three   105

SECTION 7:   Week Four   109

Objectives   110
Weekly Activity Plan   110
Business Development   110
Business Support   119
Your Next Step   119

SECTION 8:   Getting Leads   123

Standard Methods for Getting Leads   125
Other Methods for Getting Leads   128

SECTION 9:   Seven Critical Sales Skills for Success   133

Seven Critical Sales Skills   134
Sales Skill 1: Craft a Sales Call   135
Sales Skill 2: Attach a Benefit   137
Sales Skill 3: Ask a Question to Get the Order   138
Sales Skill 4: Use the AAA Method of Objection-Busting   138
Sales Skill 5: Use the "Hum" Technique   139
Sales Skill 6: Tie Down Your Benefit   141
Sales Skill 7: Discover the Motive That Drives the Decision   141

SECTION 10: **Sellers and Buyers 145**

SECTION 11: **Walking Through a Sample Business Plan 151**

SECTION 12: **Forms to Create Your Own Plan 161**

References 167

Index 170

P R E F A C E

Up and Running in 30 Days is dedicated to all the agents who have taught me "what works."

I have enjoyed helping great salespeople launch their careers to high profitability—quickly. Up and Running is organized to help you do the same.

In *Up and Running* you have a personal, detailed, workable business-development plan. It has taken me two decades in real estate sales, management, and training to organize and prioritize this business—so that you won't have to.

With *Up and Running* you can start your career today, using the same activities top producers use to create multimillion-dollar careers. Congratulations on choosing to become a dedicated, professional, successful salesperson. Before you know it, you will be serving as a success story for the industry!

INTRODUCTION

Up and Running in 30 Days has been designed as a jump-start business planning system for the novice real estate agent. A quick, successful entry into the real estate field is essential, as most new agents expect a sale within the first month. I became aware of this expectation while interviewing hundreds of new agents for *How about a Career in Real Estate?* (For more information on this book, see the Reference section.) Although most agents interviewed expressed high expectations, most didn't know what activities were necessary to achieve their goals. No one had explained to them how sales works or given them an effective start-up plan. That's like telling someone to play a Beethoven sonata without any sheet music!

Why This Book Was Written—and What It Means to Your Success

Over the years quite a few books have been written on how to achieve success in real estate sales. Most of these have offered profiles of successful real estate people.

Simply knowing what other people did to become successful won't get you on track to success, however. Each successful salesperson brings to real estate certain talents and skills you may not possess, and reading success stories may make your work sound all too easy. To succeed you must incorporate, and operate beyond, your previously developed talents and skills. You must use a precise, in-depth, proven activity plan—such as *Up and Running*—to jump-start each day.

For nearly 30 years I've been a real estate salesperson, manager, trainer, and speaker, and over the years I've seen many—too many—new agents fail for lack of a start-up plan. Prior to entering real estate management, to achieve success in real estate sales (top 2 percent) I followed a plan akin to *Up and Running.* While I didn't know it as the complete plan presented in this book, I did intuit immediately that to become successful I would need to talk to many people to find some who wanted to buy homes. Keeping this in mind, I was able to sell 40 homes during my first full year in real estate, compared with the two homes/agent sold by many of my colleagues.

As a new agent, at first I honestly didn't know why I was succeeding, but as I began observing the activities of low-producing agents, I noticed they spent most of their time *previewing properties* to "know the inventory." In contrast, my primary priority was *finding and showing homes to buyers.* I, too, viewed plenty of homes—but took genuine buyers with me to see them. For some in the real estate field, the main activity consists of previewing properties. For others, most real estate activities involve locating, working with, and closing buyers and sellers. It stands to reason that to become financially successful in real estate, you must *sell* homes, *not just preview* them.

It's Never Too Late to Get a Plan

Over the past year I have been conducting an informal survey. Every time I meet agents who have been in the real estate business for less than two years, I ask them what start-up plan they used to launch their businesses. No one has mentioned any plan other than *Up and Running in 30 Days.*

If you are an experienced agent but haven't implemented an effective business-generating plan such as *Up and Running,* you need to learn the concepts in this program before you can take your business to the next level. I have found that agents who have been in the business months to years appreciate the concepts in *Up and Running* as much as new agents, especially if they have not been achieving their goals. They, too, are anxious for a proven plan of action.

Managers have an obligation to advise agents that a start-up plan is critical to success in real estate sales. Without such advice, new agents are at an extreme disadvantage from the first day they enter the field. Without a plan, new agents just do whatever occurs to them each day—even though "shooting from the hip" never works.

All Agents Need a Business-Producing Plan— and a Coach—to Succeed

Be sure you understand that as a real estate agent you are in *sales*. To earn a reasonable income you must find prospects *yourself*. To succeed in this quest, you not only need a business-producing plan—you need a guide or coach for that plan. Not only will the plan and coach help you get off to the best start possible—to find prospects and make money—they will also help keep you on track as you locate your prospects. Just as piano students need coaching to guide them in their quest for keyboard mastery, real estate agents need coaching from seasoned professionals to help them refine technique, correct their mistakes, and encourage them to take increasingly larger risks. Finding a coach—ideally, your manager or someone trained to coach—to guide you in your business start-up will benefit you greatly both immediately and throughout your career.

Keep in mind that along with the plan and the coach comes *follow-through*. The best plan and coach will do you no good if you fail to take action; again, be sure you understand that you are in *sales* and must find prospects *yourself* to earn a reasonable income. I leapt at the opportunity to take over the management of the real estate office I sold for—thinking that I could help others become as successful as I had been. I blithely taught classes, coached agents in their business plans, and expected results. I found, however, that about half of the agents not only didn't want to incorporate any business start-up plan—they had little intention of following through after they had been coached on how to sell. These people wanted to invest their time in previewing pretty houses, not *selling* them. That experience proved to me that many agents who go into real estate either don't know what "sales" means, or simply don't intend to go out and find prospects. Such an attitude doesn't work—and people with that attitude don't last very long.

Prospective Agents May Get Off-Track—Even Before They Start

Prospective agents may get off-track even before they become active in real estate. Again, this is because few prospective agents understand what "sales" actually means. I have observed, moreover, that during the interview process many managers do not adequately explain what activities are involved in sales. These managers tend to sidetrack the issue by telling new agents that they can earn "thousands of dollars" in the business or they will do well because they have "great personalities"—or refer to the income levels of top-producing agents as if those were standard, all the while implying that little personal effort will be required to achieve financial success. It sounds as though the interviewee is so exceptional that all the interviewee will have to do is show up, get business cards—then earn $400,000 a year!

During interviews conducted for *How about a Career in Real Estate?* (see the Reference section) agents related incredible reasons why they thought they would make huge amounts of money in real estate sales. Many of these reasons were the result of talks with managers. Rarely do these managers mention to interviewees *how* these incomes are generated—and, in some cases, I doubt the managers know. Some managers simply don't think in terms of business start-up plans, and other managers are convinced success is based on the luck of the draw. That is, some agents do well and some don't—and there's nothing the manager can do to help agents start up successfully.

Managers complain that if they are honest about sales activities, agents won't join their companies. But if a new agent joins a company, believing that somehow prospects will materialize but they don't, the new agent will become depressed. The manager will step in and try to change the agent's attitude—called "motivating the agent," which doesn't work—or will become impatient, issue ultimatums, and create an adversarial situation. Such a scenario is also useless. But if managers would be honest with interviewees—and provide them an effective start-up plan before hiring them—much of the confusion and frustration that stem from the realities of real estate sales would be eliminated.

Myth: The Company Training Program Is Enough

Many real estate companies offer training programs. One myth of real estate folklore is that these "training" programs can take the place of a start-up plan. Nevertheless, it has become clear to me that few company training programs offer valuable training. I have found three problems with standard real estate company training programs:

1. These programs are not taught as "training"—they are taught as "education."
2. These programs are not centered on "sales"—they focus on the technical aspects of real estate.

3. These programs are not driven by a business-producing start-up plan.

Consider the first problem. The difference between "training" and "education" is significant. "Training" is *active* and involves *immediate practice* of what you have seen demonstrated. "Education" is essentially *passive.* Although some high schools and university colleges incorporate off-campus paraprofessional placement programs into their curricula, in most educational institutions the pattern is to file into a large room, sit down, and listen passively to the instructor review and explain a topic. Rather than learning how to *do* something, you learn *about* something. It is then up to you to take those ideas and implement them as skills in the real world. But when your learning is only passive, the instructor is the only one who knows how to do what is being taught. This is why the business world is often dissatisfied with the experience high school and college students bring to the work place. Businesses such as real estate firms are faced with training new employees from the ground up. Then, when training is offered, it tends to follow the passive "education" model, even though it is called "training." With no practice during such training, as a new agent you may, for example, hear plenty about the principles of agency—but be stumped when it comes to explaining those principles to a buyer.

The second problem is that the bulk of real estate training deals with the technical aspects of real estate, not with sales itself. Typically, modules follow this schedule:

1. Writing purchase and sale agreements
2. Completing listing agreements
3. Inspections
4. The closing process
5. Appraisals
6. Agency law

While knowledge of these subjects is crucial, it forms only part of the picture. Attending educational sessions to learn numerous facts and figures will never ensure success. You may develop a false sense of confidence that, because you know a lot, you will do well. This illusion will be quickly shattered when you discover you must talk to people to sell homes—yet you don't know what to say when you talk to them. Participating in a real estate training series is essential to helping you jump-start in the field. But in this series you should be practicing critical *sales* skills until you master them. *Up and Running* describes these critical sales skills; an effective training program demonstrates how to use them, coaching you to mastery.

The third problem is that many "training" programs consist merely of topics; they are not driven by a business-producing start-up plan. Such programs have no rhyme or reason for their organization, except that managers say they want their agents to know about the topics covered. But a valuable training program is really "on the job" training organized around a business start-up plan. In every session, the student reports back on the business start-up plan and practices the new skills to be applied to real life the following week. By the end of the series, the student should have mastered the following:

1. Implementing and measuring the results of the business start-up plan
2. The sales skills introduced in the series
3. The technical aspects of the business—and the skills needed to explain these aspects to buyers and sellers, gained by in-class practice

Time for practice and time between practices are critical for skills mastery. Mastering skills takes spaced repetition over time. An effective training program—such as *Advantage,* an action-focused, spaced repetition training created around *Up and Running*—will include practice in each session, and space between sessions so the student can absorb the new skills. (See the Reference section for more information on *Advantage.*)

Supporting Your Goals with an Effective Training Program

In the survey to new agents, I learned they expected to make a sale within their first month. If your goal is to make money fast, you need a training program that does more than provide you technical information—it needs to include sales skills practice and business start-up plan monitoring. If you can't find a training program that has the three attributes listed above, you must implement your own business start-up plan and find a coach with whom to practice—as soon as you enter real estate. Otherwise, you will spend your time *learning about* real estate, not *selling* it. This is a common pattern that you can avoid with proper planning.

To determine the constraints of company training programs, ask the managers with whom you're interviewing to show you—not just talk about—the outline, objectives, and curricula for their training programs. Please take the time to study the program. If possible, visit the classroom. Joining a company truly dedicated to your sales success and securing the best start available are critical to your career.

Identifying a Poor Plan—to Stay Away From

By now, I hope you are convinced you need to use a business start-up plan. But watch out—there are more poor ones than good ones "out there." *Poor plans*

- *Do not* prioritize activities
- *Do not* prioritize actions correctly (some actions shouldn't even be included!)
- *Do not* accentuate sales, focusing on technical aspects instead
- *Do not* have methods of setting goals, keeping track of results, and analyzing results to make changes quickly
- *Do* model themselves after a slow-starting agent, focusing, for example, on "seeing all the inventory" before doing anything else
- *Do* use outmoded methods of selling, accentuating closing techniques instead of relationship, consulting, and questioning skills
- *Do* include plenty of "busy work"—like a broker having an agent visit a title company to learn how it operates—so the broker doesn't have to spend time training the agent.

Don't think such old-fashioned ideas are gone. While writing this edition I scanned the contents of a recently published text for new agents. The table of contents include "How to Close Buyers" and "Six Traditional Closes"—but consulting, qualifying and interviewing buyers makes closing them a non-issue; concentrating on closing buyers creates manipulative, old-fashioned sales techniques that consumers have learned to hate. It also includes a chapter on "Product Knowledge"—again, the focus is on previewing pretty houses, which doesn't necessarily *sell* them. People draw conclusions based on the amount and prioritization of information they acquire. If you were a new agent, you might likely believe from the contents of that text that memorizing, using manipulative closing techniques, and looking at homes are the keys to real estate success. That's simply not the case.

What Agents Do Without a Business Plan

It's hard to say which is worse—a poor plan or no plan at all. With no plan, agents do what comes easily. As most people are afraid of rejection, they avoid activities that invite rejection, the very sales activities that produce income. Minus a plan, agents choose activities that allow them to get organized—all day; attend classes—all day; preview properties—all week; and observe others—all week. A friend notes that such agents seem to be "getting ready to get ready." The danger in creating a daily plan without good business start-up principles is creating habits of failure. Once an agent falls into the "getting ready to get ready" pattern—guaranteed to seriously hamper sales—it becomes a business plan that is difficult to change.

Identifying an Effective Plan

A poor business start-up plan is fairly easy to identify. So is an effective business start-up plan. A useful real estate business start-up plan has several features:

1. An organized activities schedule with certain activities prioritized first
2. An organized activities schedule with certain activities prioritized *second*—and explaining why
3. A road map for a continuing plan

The activities that are highest in priority are those that result in a sale or listing sold. In these activities the agent finds, interviews, chooses, works with, and sells to real estate buyers (and sellers, as the case may be). These activities are specifically *prospecting, presenting/showing,* and *closing.*

Business-Producing Activities Get Highest Priority

In *Up and Running,* business-producing activities are termed *business development* activities. These activities, which top agents call "dollar-productive activities," should be scheduled *first.* When I began selling real estate, one of the best agents in the company told me to write at the top of my daily plan, "How will I make money today?" That was good advice. It pays to develop the "success habit."

Prioritizing Business-Supporting Activities

Activities that are not directly prospecting, presenting/showing, or closing are termed *business-supporting activities.* As you may have surmised, low-producing agents tend to focus on business-supporting activities. But as you follow the guidelines in *Up and Running,* you'll naturally learn to set your schedule toward the most useful prioritization of activities—and *fast success.* You will learn to create your daily plan consciously, recognizing the value of your activities. Remember to schedule your business-producing activities first. Then, schedule your business-supporting activities. You will find that this book naturally guides you to think successfully, and that all the activities included have been prioritized to help you build the habits of a very successful real estate agent.

Building Success Habits from Day One

It's important that a business-producing plan teaches you to think like top producers and helps you set the pace for your career. *Up and Running* meets these goals by offering

- The business-developing plan followed by top agents
- The concepts behind the plan, so you can adapt it to meet your needs
- A framework for a weekly business plan for each of your first four weeks in real estate
- The support and technical activities you should be doing your first four weeks in real estate
- Sales skills and sales calls, including a specific script

Summary: The Full Scope of *Up and Running*

This introduction has discussed some of the challenges facing those who enter the field of real estate. Among these are

- Underestimating the sales nature of real estate, often the result of misleading statements from well-meaning brokers
- Poor or non-existent training programs
- Poor or non-existent business start-up plans and a lack of coaching opportunities

Up and Running in 30 Days offers you a clear, concise, precise counter to these challenges. It shows you exactly how to create sales by the numbers, teaching you to measure success and providing reassurance that you are on target. This activity plan includes measurements and provides the basis for coaching from those who want to guide you but may have no game plan.

In *Up and Running* you get the "why." You learn *why* this business start-up plan is prioritized following the success principles of sales creation. *Up and Running* follows the "business development and business supporting activity prioritization" concept. With the "why" in mind you can continue creating effective plans long after you're not following the *Up and Running* plan to the letter.

In *Up and Running* you get the "how." *Up and Running* explains critical sales skills and sales calls so you can find a partner and practice until you have mastered these skills.

And in *Up and Running* you get the "what"—what to do each day. To help you create your business plan, *Up and Running* includes

- A full set of planning guides

- A sample business-development plan
- Business-producing assignments
- Assignments for business support
- Manager/facilitator checklist

All these elements make up the who, what, when, where, and why of a successful real estate career. Armed with this full start-up plan, and understanding the concepts behind it, you will be thinking each day like a top producer. You have ahead of you a very successful sales career!

1

Heads Up: New Trends That Will Affect How You Do Business

Real estate is changing dramatically. Since the late twentieth century seven trends have made major impact on the business of real estate sales. These trends comprise

- Evolving company structures
- Relationship marketing
- Systematization
- Technology
- Training
- Coaching
- Teaming

These trends have permanently affected real estate sales; to be successful in the field you must learn to recognize them—and embrace them in practice.

Trend Number One: Evolving Company Structures

Types of Companies

Several trends in the organization of real estate offices will determine your income and business-producing activities. The main organizational structures that have evolved in real estate offices are the *dependent* real estate company structure, the *independent* real estate company structure, and the *interdependent* real estate company structure.

The Dependent Real Estate Company Structure. In the 1970s, when I began selling real estate, an agent worked for a broker and split the commissions that came into the company 50/50 with that broker. In exchange for splitting commissions the agent did not have to spend any money on marketing or other business services. This created a relationship in which the agent was extremely dependent upon the broker for sales and success. Many companies still use this dependent company structure and make real estate agents dependent on them for marketing—and even for prospects, for which the agent pays an ever-increasing fee. These companies tend to take a paternalistic view of the company-agent relationship; that is, the company knows best and the agent needs the strength of the company. The trend inside dependent companies is to "take back the business"—to buy leads from affiliated companies, then sell these leads to agents. These companies are not very concerned about helping agents create individually powerful businesses; they are concerned about increasing their bottom lines. The end result is that the agent makes less money per transaction.

The E-company—blessing or curse to real estate? An E-company is a real estate company that generates leads via the Internet. An E-company promises leads to agents—for a healthy fee. Some E-companies are effectively changing the status of the agent from independent contractor to salary-based employee.

Keep in mind that if your leads are generated by someone else, as is the case with an E-company, you will not get paid as much as you are paid if you secure your own leads. The objective of the E-company is the same as the dependent company—to take over all the lead generation and sell those leads to lower-paid agents. Be especially careful of E-company claims about potential earnings.

The Independent Real Estate Company Structure. About 15 years ago, another organizational concept emerged in real estate—the "100 percent concept." In this concept, agents are viewed as independent, paying the company a desk fee and keeping all commission dollars. In return, the company does not provide many services. This kind of company uses an independent company structure. This structure does not attempt to help the agent create a strong business—that's up to the agent.

New agents may be drawn to the independent real estate company structure because it costs less to join. Generally, however, these companies provide no coaching, no business start-up plan, and no mentoring. Although there are exceptions—great managers who will coach new agents—to master sales quickly you must determine before joining what kind of guidance, coaching, and consulting you will receive.

The Interdependent Real Estate Company Structure. The third type of company structure emerged only about a decade ago, paralleling its introduction to business internationally. In this company structure, termed *interdependent,* the company and agent partner to create a strong business for the agent. Other structural attributes can include profit-sharing, stock options, and participatory leadership—rewards and empowerment for helping make the company successful. Real estate companies with interdependent structure specialize in training, coaching, and consulting agents to high production and effective business management. They provide these ser-vices to new agents, growing agents, and high-producing agents.

For the new agent this type of company is ideal. Training, coaching, consulting, and mutual support are available. Along with this comes accountability for putting the systems into action. Some even have web sites that teach agents how to choose a coach, how to be accountable for results, and how to set up consequences for positive and negative results.

Sadly, most real estate companies seem to have no expectations or accountability methods in place. Most measure numbers of agents and market share as signs of success—even though a company can have 1,000 agents who individually make little money and still seem a successful operation.

The interdependent company structure is gaining strength in the real estate field not only because of the training and coaching opportunities it offers new agents but because of its benefits to those more seasoned in real estate sales. An effective interdependent company offers those who have mastered the skills of real estate sales the graduate-level training and consulting necessary to master the skills of managing a business—systematizing, delegating, expanding, supporting with technology, supervising, and analyzing a budget and profit/loss statements. When choosing a real estate company, look beyond what you'll get in new agent training and evaluate how the company will teach you to grow a real business you can sell—not just create a sales career.

Choosing a Company to Fit Your Career Goals

Too often agents choose a company based on how much of the commission they will be allowed to keep. That's like always choosing to drive a particular car model because it's the cheapest available. If you want a real career, you need to choose a company dedicated to helping you reach your professional and personal goals.

The *Up and Running* start-up plan presented in this book works best when you are with a company that takes an individual approach to helping you create a singular, dynamic business. You'll find that company by investigating its commitment to "action focus" training—skills practice and action plans with high accountability for achievement. That company should make clear to you that your success comes first.

By examining *Up and Running*, you will see that none of your success depends on leads your company provides you. Neither you nor the company can guarantee those leads; but by working *Up and Running* and increasing your skill you will create a powerful business. Choose your company, your office, and your manager to coach and support the goals in this business start-up plan—whether your relationship to your company is dependent, independent, or interdependent.

Trend Number Two: Relationship Marketing

Relationship marketing is the key to cutting your expenses and increasing your effectiveness. It involves creating deep professional bonds with clients, so that you earn the right to return and referral business.

Agents used to be able to get away with an "order taker attitude": sell a house, then wait for the next buyer. While great agents didn't operate that way—they practiced relationship marketing—it was still possible to make some money being an order taker. Those days are over.

No longer is the agent's job just to sell—it's also to relate. Successful real estate demands a firm commitment; it takes at least three years to build a career, and your clients expect you to commit to their best interests for the long term.

The concepts in *Up and Running* support relationship marketing. You will see that your prospecting plan, explained in Section 2, begins with your best source of prospects—people you know and meet. Later on, this "best source" becomes your former clients. If you begin with this concept now, you will keep building your best source, as top agents do. I will be referring to the concept of relationship marketing throughout this book.

Trend Number Three: Systematization

To be more effective you need to "duplicate and delegate." It's impossible to create much of a real estate business today without creating checklists for all processes and systems for each part of your business. This includes checklists for pre-listing and pre-selling packages, and sellers' and buyers' presentations as well as new listing and post-sale checklists.

Years ago I became tired of selling "by the seat of my pants" and began to create checklists for all the processes I had to complete. I found I could move much faster and delegate more effectively when I followed a checklist. Systematizing your real estate business is essential; there are more details, legalities, and responsibilities than ever before.

A number of publications include checklists. Among these are *The Real Estate Agent's Business Planning Guide*, *On Track to Success in 30 Days*, and the training program *Advantage*. For more information on these publications, see the Reference section.

Checklists are certainly helpful. Keep in mind, though, that it's best to organize as you go. Spending the bulk of your energy on organization prior to prospecting may give you an orderly office—but cost you sales. It's talking to people that makes sales, not neatness.

Trend Number Four: Technology

As a new agent, I was handed a recipe card box and recipe cards and advised to keep all my prospect and client names on those cards. Although recipe and card files are passe, when you go into your office you probably will still observe some agents trying to keep track of all the names they gather on scraps of paper and in card files.

Use technology to support your dynamic business! The easiest way to organize the names of prospects and clients is on a computer. If you're not in the technology world now—jump in. You'll need technology to do the following:

1. Organize your prospects, clients, and affiliates (such as mortgage lenders) in a database
2. Organize your follow-up programs for specific target markets via a contact management program

3. Create your business and distribution plans—how you'll keep in contact with past customers, for example—and implement them

4. Keep in contact with your customers via cellphone and pager

5. Carry your contacts (database), schedule, and so on with you on a personal digital assistant

6. Create a personal web page that promotes you and/or provides your prospects and clients access to information they value, such as updates on their property, marketing, or transaction progress

7. Take pictures and add them to your web page and flyers via a digital camera

8. Find properties and prepare seller and buyer presentations on your own computer

9. Budget for your expenses, track expenses, and create, implement, and analyze your profit and loss statements

These include only a few of the technologies agents use in business. Before you buy anything, interview three technology-savvy, high-producing agents in your office and identify the technologies they consider important. Create a priority list, with dates and budget, to buy and learn these technologies. Don't expect your real estate company to provide them, although seasoned agents within your organization may be willing to provide direction on the best use of technology. Sections of this book will remind you how to use technology to work effectively with your start-up plan. Several books— among them *The Hottest e-careers in Real Estate* and *Terri Murphy's e-Listing and e-Selling Secrets for the Technologically Clueless*, also by published by Dearborn™ Real Estate Education—can help you use technology wisely.

Keep in mind, though, that people want to be sold homes by people, not by computers. Don't hide behind your computer learning new technologies. Don't think you're going to be successful because you know more about e-mail than anyone else. And don't judge start-up plans such as *Up and Running* as less than complete because they don't include details on all the latest technology. What matters is that you stay with the start-up plan, adding your improvisations as you go.

Trend Number Five: Training

There are three trends in real estate training today:

1. Some companies have abandoned training and expect agents to survive on provided leads for dollars.

2. Some companies provide action-focused training in both sales and graduate business areas.

3. Some companies rely on "distance learning" to train agents.

These trends are heading in opposite directions and producing opposite results.

Abandoning—or Accelerating—Training

Let's take the first two trends together. While the real estate business is a classic sales career, it has become much more complicated by regulations and the need for technologies. It's easy for a new agent to get off track; training, coaching, and partnering all help an agent stay focused.

Through the 1990s, many large franchises dropped much of their sales training. The training programs of these franchises could not measure sales results, so these franchises felt the cost of trainers and programs wasn't justified. Moreover, most new agents were not making enough money for the franchises to justify spending thousands of dollars on the new agents.

Are companies right in downscaling their training programs? Think of what the rest of the business world is doing. They're *not down-scaling*—they're *improving* their training programs. Real estate consumers expect agents to provide a continually increasing level of service. Without effective, action-focused sales training, that won't happen.

Many of the now-extinct training programs offered by franchises were ineffective because they didn't offer true "training"—they offered education. To get results, real estate training programs must change focus. These changes must occur in:

1. Student accountability—Students must be expected to perform sales and support activities with a particular level of quality.
2. Training program content and instruction methods—In addition to technical information, content and methods must involve education/lecture methods and interactive, role-play, case study, and action plan methods focusing on sales plans and skills.

Although the "training" that some companies offer is more of a recruiting tool than an effective start-up plan, a few organizations are truly dedicated to individual professional development. One of the best times to determine whether a real estate company has a genuinely useful training program is during your interview. As questions such as:

- What are the students required to achieve during the training program? (See the schedule of required activity completion, so you'll know exactly what is expected of you.)
- How does the instructor know the students met these goals?
- How is competency measured? Who measures it?

- What will this program do for me as an agent? (Does it start you up in your sales activities or does it just give you technical information?)

Few real estate companies today can claim that their core competency—where they really excel—is training. By asking these questions, you'll be able to choose a company on these terms.

Beyond Sales Training to Business Creation and Management

Training is a continuous process. It certainly should *not* end once the new agent has become established. The most progressive companies today offer training to their agents in each phase of their careers, including graduate-level courses. Forward-thinking companies help agents work on their business—planning, budgeting, analyzing profit/loss, creating buyers' agents, managing staff, and so on. If you want to create a dynamic, long-term career, look for a company with dedicated, sophisticated resources and expertise, and a comprehensive program for continuous professional growth.

Distance Learning: Jump-Start Tool?

Distance learning via audio, video, and interactive computer is a continuing educational trend. In this form of education, the instructor is not in the room with you. You can take courses anywhere and you can learn at your own speed. Distance learning is being touted in the business world as a wonderful solution to travel expenses, limited time, the desire for people to learn—fast.

But consider this: Much of what we learn we learn through time and practice. Distance learning can't provide the coaching, feedback, accountability, and hands-on experience you need to get you started fast. I learned to sell real estate by doing it, not through distance learning, just as I learned to perform musically with a piano coach who constantly urged me to strive toward mastery. Use distance learning as an additional tool—not the solution to your training needs.

Several educational Internet sites can help you refine your business. One of these, www.isucceed.com, offers ideas every month, from about 200 real estate agents. Remember, though, that computer learning is no substitute for business-plan-centered, get-into-action training—live.

Trend Number Six: Coaching

"Coaching" Defined

Companies that specialize in high-level training also tend to specialize in coaching. Coaching is a highly particular, directive, one-on-one relationship in which the coach

1. directs action following a particular, pre-agreed on plan, and
2. holds the person coached accountable to that particular, pre-agreed on game plan.

Does everyone in real estate sales need a coach? Often new agents think they need a coach because they must have all the *answers* to succeed. They wrongly consider a coach an "answer man." These agents are correct in that they won't have all the answers—but no agent I have ever known failed from lack of answers. What agents do need to succeed is *direction.* A coach can help an agent with direction—what to do daily, how to implement a plan, and how to measure success.

Some real estate companies that claim they offer training also claim they offer coaching. They likewise claim to offer mentoring. The term *mentoring* is problematic, for it implies that the mentor provides answers, not direction. Many mentoring programs are simply "You ask, I answer" situations—hardly the setting to encourage individual professional development. Although the real estate industry claims to offer the proper tools for individual professional development, the reality falls short for two reasons:

1. The new agent—as well as the experienced agent—underestimates the need for expert training, coaching, and consulting.
2. The real estate owner, manager, and trainer underestimate the need to create excellent, masterful, accountability-based programs.

Choosing a Coach

In searching for a real estate coach, watch for these indicators:

1. The specific program should be in a handbook, precisely outlined with checklists and systems, similar to a game book.
2. The specific program should be related to a "game plan"—a business start-up plan.
3. The coaches should be trained and coached themselves.

The trend toward training and coaching is emerging in the companies most dedicated to agent success. Nevertheless, many companies still are not improving their training programs. If agents are not encouraged to develop their professional skills—or supported in their efforts through excellent training and coaching—consumers will reduce the amount of money they are willing to pay for services rendered.

Trend Number Seven: Teaming

Years ago, when agents paid 50 percent of their total commissions to their companies, their companies paid all expenses. The picture has changed. Companies generally give the agent more of the commission dollar, commonly on a sliding scale. The more income the agent brings to the company, the larger percentage of that income the agent keeps. Some retain no commissions; instead, they charge desk and other fees to pay their operating costs and make a profit. Because these companies keep less of the total commission dollar, they pay for much less—or nothing.

During this period companies did not need to charge for "lead procurement"—that is, attracting a buyer or seller through marketing. Such a lead was given free to the agents. Now more and more companies are charging for leads; for example, a lead from a company's relocation division costs an agent 35 to 45 percent.

Teaming helps agents obtain leads as they start up business. While agents earn the most in commission dollars when they generate their leads themselves, a new agent may need to pay for someone else's lead generation to begin to develop business. A number of high-producing agents, often called "rainmakers," have great lead procurement businesses, spending many of their own marketing dollars to generate leads they parcel out to their "teams." This certainly helps a new agent earn income rapidly. There is a downside to this approach, however. Agents can become complacent and sit and wait for leads. Moreover, agents who wait for leads will not start their own business development plans—until they get tired of paying for someone else's leads.

If you are considering becoming part of a team, find out whether you can sell and list houses outside the team—and how much the team leader would charge you if you did. Read the contract the team leader asks you to sign and be sure you understand the consequences of your involvement.

The seven trends presented in this Section will be referred to throughout this book. Armed with knowledge of these trends, you will be "heads up" as you begin your career. Now, let's move on to the *Up and Running* business development concepts, presented in Section 2.

2

The Five Principles of a High-Producing Business

Too often new agents receive an activity plan without an explanation of the principles behind the plan. To get your business off to a fast start and keep it on track for the long term, you need to understand and apply the *five principles of creating a high-producing business:*

1. Start the business cycle by talking to people.
2. Stay on the business path.
3. Prioritize your activities.
4. Prospect like the pros.
5. Work the numbers.

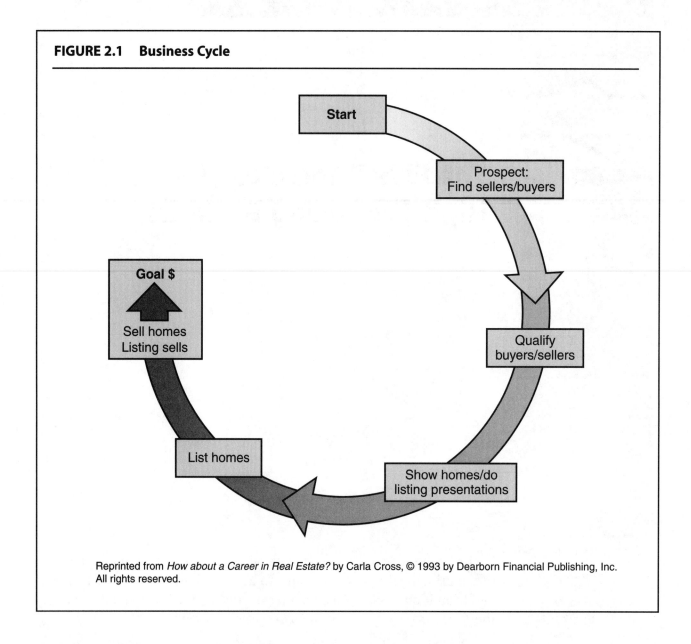

FIGURE 2.1 Business Cycle

Principle One: Start the Business Cycle

The most important principle in the activity plan is this: Business starts when you start talking to people.

> *"…the only message that needs to be stressed is to prospect a major portion of your day. Get the scripts and dialogues needed to cold call, door knock, work expireds and FSBOs. Do the work, and you'll become a great, consistently high-producing agent."*
>
> —Rick Franz, third-year top-producing agent

To be successful quickly, the most important activity you need to accomplish every day—*at least four hours a day—is to talk to people to get a lead.* This activity starts the business cycle (see Figure 2.1).

The more often you talk to people, the greater your chances to continue the business cycle, to work with and sell someone a property. *Up and Running* will ensure that you spend enough time in the sales cycle to reach your monetary expectations.

Principle Two: Stay on the Business Path

"If you don't prospect, the potential for failing in this business greatly increases. I wish I knew how to tell other agents, in a nice way, to get the hell out of my way when they try to discourage me from proactive prospecting!"
—Brian Orvis, first-year, top-producing agent

Your objective in real estate sales is to get on the *business path* and to stay on it every day until you get to the end of the road—a sale or a listing sold. Figure 2.2 illustrates the business path.

Seems simple, doesn't it? However, many obstacles get in the way—anxiety over making sales calls, fear of not knowing enough, dread of rejection, need for more organization, quest for more knowledge—the list is endless. *Up and Running* will help you stay on the business path, while filling some of those other needs in the correct relationship to your mission—to *sell real estate.*

Principle Three: Prioritize Your Activities

"What I would have given to have had a job description indicating a plan of attack. For example, this is how your day must be scheduled: prospecting three hours, follow-up, clerical, etc."
—Rick Franz, now a very successful agent, formerly in hotel management

It's all here, Rick, in *Up and Running*—the hours, the prioritizations, and the concepts behind the schedule. First and foremost, you must spend at least four hours a day starting the sales cycle. Where do the other activities fit in? To teach the habits of successful agents, this system has been prioritized for you. As you plan each day, you'll see that your activities fall under two categories:

1. *Business Development* (activities in the sales cycle)
   - Contacting prospects
   - Following up on leads

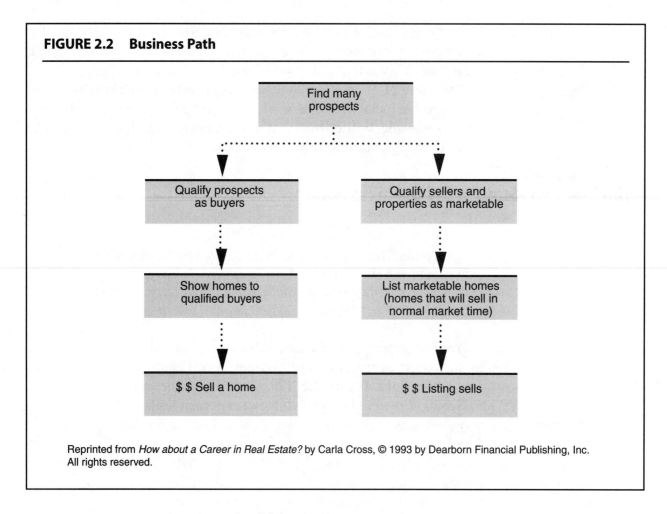

FIGURE 2.2   Business Path

- Qualifying buyers
- Showing homes to qualified prospects
- Writing and presenting offers to purchase
- Giving listing presentations to qualified sellers
- Listing marketable properties
- Attending offer presentations on your listings

2. ***Business Support*** (activities that support the sales activities)
   - Previewing properties
   - Following up on transactions, making flyers, etc.
   - Sending out mailings (should not be considered a prime contact method)
   - Talking to loan officers and title companies
   - Attending meetings
   - Furthering education
   - Creating listing manuals

This list could be exhaustive. It's common for agents to "hide out" in support activities because they think they are not ready to talk to people. Watch out. This is a sign of creating the *wrong* activities in

FIGURE 2.3   Prototype Schedule

Time Commitments: How to allocate your time to ensure quick success.

Activity	Daily	No./Week	Hours
Business development plan (prospecting)	4 hours	5 days	20
Open house		Once a week\	3–4
Floor time (if scheduled)		1 day	3
Business meeting	1 hour	Once a week	1
Office education	1 hour	1 day	1
Manager/agent counseling		Once a week	1–2
Previewing homes	2 hours	5 days	10

Schedule

Mon.	8:00 - 8:45	Meet with manager Paperwork/calls
	8:45 - 9:30	Business meeting
	9:30 - 12:30	New office listing tour
	Lunch	
	1:30 - 5:30	Business plan (prospecting)
Tues.	Day off—take it!!	
Wed.	8:00 - 9:00	Paperwork
	9:00 - 10:00	Business plan (prospecting)
	10:00 - 12:00	Previewing
	1:00 - 5:00	Business plan (prospecting)
Thurs.	8:00 - 9:00	Paperwork
	9:00 - 11:00	Previewing
	12:00 - 3:00	Floor time/buyer tour
	3:00 - 6:00	Business plan (prospecting)
Fri.	8:00 - 8:45	Paperwork
	8:45 - 9:15	Office class
	9:30 - 12:00	Previewing
	1:00 - 5:00	Business plan (prospecting)
	7:00 - 8:00	Listing presentation
Sat.	9:00 - 12:00	Business plan (prospecting)
	1:00 - 4:00	Listing presentation/buyer tour
	4:00 - 5:00	Paperwork
Sun.	12:00 - 2:00	Business plan (prospecting)
	2:00 - 5:00	Open house or buyer tour
	5:00 - 6:00	Listing presentation

the business plan. These agents could end up becoming their own assistants—or someone else's!

Prioritized for You

This book is arranged to help you keep these activities in the right perspective. Each week, the business-producing activities are assigned first—the same way a successful agent plans a week. Figure 2.3 illustrates a prototype schedule that shows how much time you should be spending on each category. Use this schedule to check against the actual plan you design each week.

Principle Four: Prospect Like the Pros

One of the foundations of *Up and Running* is the *30 Days to Dollars* prospecting plan. This plan is built on the solid prospecting principles that make real estate superstars successful. It uses the same target markets (sources of business) and numbers that superstars rely on to build a professional career. To create a high-number, highly profitable career, superstars:

- secure at least 50 percent of their business from people they know (called *referrals*).
- gain business by promoting themselves on their successes.
- devise the particular prospecting program that meets their monetary and personality needs.
- secure the majority of their business through proactive prospecting. (They find people—they don't wait for people to come to them.)

But you're not a superstar yet. *30 Days to Dollars* takes the superstars' business-development principles and translates them to your situation:

- *Work your best source of prospects.* At this point, you have no past customers. But you do have a great network of people you know. Start with them.
- *Promote success.* Next, superstars create more success by promoting their success. If you are a new agent, find someone in your office who will let you promote yourself on his or her success—a new listing taken, a sale, a listing sold, an open house. This method is called *circle prospecting.* (Refer to Section 8 for an explanation of this process.)
- *Choose a prospecting method that matches your style.* Superstars create their own unique methods of prospecting based on their

personality styles and relationships. You can, too. The *30 Days to Dollars* plan provides several methods for meeting prospects. (Refer to Section 8 for more information on these methods.)

30 Days to Dollars translates these concepts that successful agents use to create ever-high-producing businesses to your situation, so that you can create the same kind of career base—quickly.

What about Cold Calling?

Cold calling means picking up the phone, dialing a stranger and asking for a lead. Although cold calling is the quickest way to get a lead, it isn't the most common way successful agents re-create their businesses. The *30 Days to Dollars* plan, which does not include cold calls, is modeled after the *best sources* of business. You start with the best source of prospects—people who already know you. Remember: *The warmer the relationship, the better chance you have of getting a lead.*

Your long-term goal is to create relationships that, over time, will deliver back referrals to you. Warm calling does a better job of creating those relationships.

What Works.   Too often agents want someone to give them a prospecting method that is guaranteed to work. However, what always works is: *The numbers.*

Cold calling does provide more contacts in the least amount of time. But it also brings more rejections and tougher contacts to convert. So, if you run out of people to talk to in the target markets recommended in *30 Days to Dollars,* go ahead and make cold calls—to anyone—using any method you want.

A Script for Cold Calling.   A sales skill called *how to craft a sales call* is described in Section 6. Using this technique, you can craft a sales call to any target market. If you want to cold call in an area, just put together a script using this crafting technique. You will become a master cold caller because you not only have a script, you have the methodology behind the script.

If You Don't Know Anyone.   If you are new to your area, you will need to start with colder calls. However, before you begin cold calling, take another look at the people you come in contact with weekly. I'll bet you know more people than you think. Make a list of the service people you meet each week. Remember, every time you talk to someone, find out if they have a real estate need. Some of my best leads have been from my hairdresser!

Look at cold calling this way: It increases your "repertoire". Being able to make several kinds of sales calls, and mastering the sales skills in this program assures you have the repertoire. In jazz, we called being able to keep up with anyone we played with "chops". Our favorite question when thinking of hiring someone to work with us was, "Does he/she have the necessary 'chops'?"

But I Don't Wanna!   Of course you don't want to do certain types of prospecting. Don't restrict yourself to only one type of prospecting—unless it is paying off big from the beginning. Develop the 'chops' so you have them when you need them.

It Won't Work for Me in My Area.   Of course it won't. If you think you can follow only what's on the written page, you are wrong. I am giving you the template, the process, and the system. I'm giving you enough information for you to get started. You can improvise on this tune. The principles here are proven; this is a system. Use it as a basis to improvise. After you prove it, teach it to others.

Remember the "Relationship Marketing" Trend

Your business start-up is based on the trend—and the marketing truism—that relationship marketing creates the most business in the shortest amount of time, with the least cost. In fact, relationship marketing has always been the method great salespeople use to create long-term business. Businesses internationally have discovered that it is the best way to market their businesses because it costs less and delivers better results.

An example of how companies have changed their strategy and their training is in how car salespeople treat customers. A good car salesman today actually keeps in touch with you after you have bought the car! Although that used to be rare, it's more common today because car company surveys have showed that people buy the same car again not because of mechanical service excellence but because they feel the people in the car dealership cared for them.

How many agents do you think keep in contact with the buyer and seller after the sale? Not many. Agents still think that their job is to find strangers and sell them something, then move on to the next stranger. Remember, it's nine times more expensive to advertise to find strangers (like ads in newspapers), than it is to keep the old customer and get referrals.

Applying the Systematization Trend to Relationship Marketing.
Don't think that you can keep your relationships by ignoring the people

FIGURE 2.4   Systemize Your Relationship Marketing

Name	Date to re-call	Date to send mail	What to send
_____	_____	_____	_____
_____	_____	_____	_____
_____	_____	_____	_____
_____	_____	_____	_____
_____	_____	_____	_____
_____	_____	_____	_____
_____	_____	_____	_____
_____	_____	_____	_____

you have talked to. You must create a marketing plan to "re-touch" them regularly. Right now: Make a simple plan to keep in touch with all the people you will be meeting. Here's an outline, in Figure 2.4, of what you'll want in the plan.

Now you're systematizing your relationship cultivation. It's impossible to remember all these dates if you are doing this whenever you think of it. Instead, create a simple system—a marketing plan—to keep in touch with the people you have started relationships with.

You may be wondering, "What will I say when I call?" Make up something! Ask the people how their children, dogs, cars, jobs, etc. are doing. It doesn't matter what you ask them. What matters is that you cared enough to keep in touch.

Many companies will provide postcards and mailing services to keep in touch. See your manager or company catalog for lists of these companies and services. You can easily create a call/postcard program to let these people know you care about them. If you prefer creating a program yourself, see senior agents in your office. They can help you create simple postcards with current or sold listings. You can also send flyers or brochures of homes you've recently listed and sold. At first, your list will be small, so write a personal note on each mailing to let the buyers and sellers know you are thinking about them. For in-depth information about marketing, see *The Real Estate Agent's Business Planning Guide,* listed in the References section.

Applying Technology Trends to Relationship Marketing.   How will you remember these details? Apply another trend. Buy and use a contact management program. These can range from sales contact management programs to specific real estate programs. Check with the agents in your office for common use. The technology "gurus" tell us that the biggest deterrent to using technology is learning it. If you are using a program that a few of the agents in your office use, you can solve your usage problems together.

What to keep track of:

- All of the person's contact data, including e-mail and Web page information. It's especially important today to get e-mail addresses so that you can send updates and newsletters via e-mail.
- Personal preferences and personal information, such as birthdays, dogs, children's names, etc.
- Information regarding each transaction.

Real estate-specific programs already have these "fields" built into their programs, so, for a person new to real estate or databases, these customized databases are useful. The downside is that the real-estate specific programs are more expensive.

Two other bonuses that real estate specific programs offer are

1. Letters for many contact occasions
2. Marketing plans for specific target markets (identifiable groups of people with common needs)—such as people selling their own homes "for sale by owners") or people who have tried to sell their homes through real estate agents but failed ("expired listings")

A fellow board member of an Internet training company that specializes in on-line real estate training—and who is a founder of the largest contact management software company for real estate professionals—tells me that agents who buy his programs use only a fraction of the features. He also gives an example of a top-producing agent who closes about $20 million of properties a year and has been lauded for his innovating marketing programs. In fact, all this agent is doing is using the programs provided in his software!

As a new agent, unless you are very contact-management savvy and have been in sales before, I caution you against using a generic contact management program. Instead, buy real-estate specific software and learn all the features. Use the letters and marketing programs in the software, until you are comfortable customizing them and/or creating your own programs. Using these programs will be a self-training tool. Take advantage of the thousands of hours of expertise that went into creating those programs for real estate agents!

FIGURE 2.5   30 Days to Dollars

Each week you will have a business-producing assignment based on this prospecting plan.

Activity	Weekly Minimum
1. Contact people you know/meet.	
In-person calls	20
Phone calls	30
Follow-up (phone calls, mail, e-mail, etc.)	50
2. Circle prospect in person.	25
3. Choose one additional activity from these.	
Farm Area in-person contacts	50
or	
FSBOs in-person or phone contacts	25
or	
Expired listings in-person or phone contacts	25
4. Hold public open houses.	1

Total weekly minimum in-person/phone contacts: **100-125**

Start Your Prospecting

30 Days to Dollars (see Figure 2.5) is a daily prospecting program that will ensure a sale in your first 30 days in the business. The activities are prioritized for you, so you can create the same kind of career that the superstars develop—from day one. Each week you will have an assignment based on this plan.

Figure 2.6 provides a different view of *30 Days to Dollars*. This grid allows you to set goals and keep track of your prospecting success. This is the first step in successful business implementation—setting short-term goals and measuring the results. Using this chart:

1. choose the markets you intend to work;
2. set goals for the number of people you intend to meet within these markets; and
3. log in your "actuals" (the number of contacts you actually make) each week.

The activities listed in Figure 2.5 will lead to results. These results are listed in the Monthly Activity Scorecard (see Figure 2.7). Think of these results as merely a continuation of the sales cycle that you started with the activities in *30 Days to Dollars*.

Step-by-Step to Dollars

It's important to note that this Monthly Activity Scorecard represents the sales process in order. Many business activity lists circulated in various new-agent classes do not reflect the natural progress of the sales cycle. Poorly organized scorecards misrepresent the sales process and how certain activities predict certain results. For example, you can't sell homes unless you show them to many buyers. You can't show and sell homes unless you first qualify the buyers. This scorecard is organized to help you plan effective sales activities.

How to use this scorecard:

1. Set goals for buyer and listing activities.
2. Use the numbers in Principle Five to compare your goals with proven ratios. You may want to adjust your goals.
3. Log in your "actuals."
4. Evaluate your progress.

Principle Five: Work the Numbers

Do you want to make a sale in your first month in the business? If so, you need to make at least 100 prospecting calls (in person or on the phone) each week, for the first four weeks you're in the business. This is your *insurance plan*. The *30 Days to Dollars* plan has 100 calls per week built into the program. You will use and assess this program each week. With this method, you will learn an important *self-management tool*—the ability to measure and analyze your activities, and the results of those activities.

FIGURE 2.6   Your 30 Days to Dollars Plan (Prospecting)

Month: _____

Proactive Activities

	Week 1		Week 2		Week 3		Week 4		Totals	
	G	A	G	A	G	A	G	A	G	A
People you know/meet [50/week]										
Circle prospect [25/week]										
Farm [50/week]										
FSBOs [25/week]										
Expireds [25/week]										

Reactive Prospecting Activities

	Week 1		Week 2		Week 3		Week 4		Totals	
	G	A	G	A	G	A	G	A	G	A
Open houses [1min]										

G=Goals
A=Actuals

Proactive means you go out and find a prospect.
Reactive means you wait for a prospect to come to you.

FIGURE 2.7   Monthly Activity Scorecard (Results of Prospecting)

Month: _____

Buyer Activities	Week 1 G	Week 1 A	Week 2 G	Week 2 A	Week 3 G	Week 3 A	Week 4 G	Week 4 A	Totals G	Totals A
Counseling Appointments w/ buyers										
Qualified buyer showings										
# sales										

Listing Activities	Week 1 G	Week 1 A	Week 2 G	Week 2 A	Week 3 G	Week 3 A	Week 4 G	Week 4 A	Totals G	Totals A
Qualified listing appointments										
Marketable listings secured										
# of listings sold										

G=Goals   A=Actuals

More Numbers: High Activities Reap Rewards

Remember the sales path? Let's add some numbers to that path, so we can project the results of our prospecting efforts.

On the sales side:

- 400 sales calls per month will return to you
- 12 qualifying appointments that will result in
- 8 showings that, if averaged over time, will result in 1 sale.

This means: If you want to sell one home per month, you need to talk to 400 people in that month, find 12 people to qualify, and show homes 8 times. You will, averaged over a few months, sell 1 home for every 8 times you put people in the car (not necessarily the same people—this is just a law of averages).

On the listing side:

- *400* contacts a month will result in
- *4* seller qualifying appointments that will lead to
- *2* qualified listings of which 1 listing will sell in market time.

The *Up and Running* plan has these numbers built into each week's business-producing activities. You will set a goal for *one sale and one listing* during the first four weeks of your business. In addition, you'll be setting standards for your business that will assure you of making a good living and building a solid career—from day one.

Up and Running Puts All the Business Principles Together

With these five principles, you have the basics of successful real estate business development. In addition, *Up and Running* provides an easy way of applying these principles to your situation. The following two tools will help you to shortcut your career challenges:

1. Weekly assignments and objectives to ensure that you reach your goals
2. A sample business-development plan, developed by agent Joan Smith

Joan Smith's Plan

To help clarify these business-development concepts, take a look at new agent Joan Smith's plan. Her complete business development plan, included in Section 11, shows how she planned her weekly, monthly, and yearly goals to be successful quickly by using the principles and assignments in *Up and Running*.

Start with the Big Picture and Work to the Specifics.   Joan starts with the big picture and works to the specifics. Let's follow Joan now, as she creates her business development plan. First, using the grid on the next page, she sets her monetary goal. For Joan, that's $36,000 her first year in real estate. (This, by the way, is higher than the median income for all REALTORS® according to the latest National Association of REALTORS® survey. I'm assuming that you, unlike other REALTORS®, intend to really work at real estate in a planned way). Because the average income for the agent per sale in her market is $3,000, this means that she'll need to sell one home per month (or have one of her listings sell). In the real estate industry, each sale or listing sold is termed a "revenue unit". You will note that Joan will create one-half a revenue unit per month from a sale and a listing sold.

Know the Number of Activities Needed To Get a Result.   Joan's manager has told her that it takes approximately four listing appointments to list one home that sells in normal market time. It takes eight showing appointments to sell one home (This means eight groups of people in the car, not numbers of homes shown. They don't even have to be different groups; it's just the law of averages). As Joan wants the result of one transaction per month, she knows she will have to put people in her car at least four times a month and go to a listing presentation four times per month to ensure that she reaches her goal. As she knows her fastest method of getting a check is through a sale, she sets a goal of eight showings per month. She also knows that her skill level isn't high at the beginning of her career, so she sets higher showing and listing presentation goals for herself than she will need to set later in her career.

Using *30 Days to Dollars* as an Activity Plan.   Note how Joan relates her monetary goals to her monthly and weekly activities (see Figure 2.8). The *30 Days to Dollars* plan suits Joan's needs. It gives her enough contacts to ensure that she reaches her goal—one sale or listing sold per month, which will result in her making her monetary goal of $36,000.

To schedule her contacts and business results for the remainder of the year, Joan follows the same contact plan she used for her third month onward. A similar planning page is illustrated in Section 12.

From Breakeven to Profitability

In order to plan your finances, you will need to complete the grid *From Breakeven to Profitability* (see Figures 2.9 and 2.10). This grid shows the

FIGURE 2.8   Joan's Yearly Goals Translated to Monthly Goals and Activities

1. Set your monthly expectations

Your $ expectations this year

$$\boxed{\$\ 36,000} \div 12 = \boxed{\$\ 3,000}$$

Monthly expectation in $

2. Translate $ to Units *
* "Units" are numbers of sales and listings sold

Monthly expectation in $ Your $ earned sale per listing sold   Monthly unit goal

$$\boxed{\$\ 3,000} \div \boxed{\$\ 3,000} = \boxed{1/2 \quad 1/2}$$

Listing sold   Sales

3. Plan activities to meet unit goals

	Month 1	2	3	4	5	6
Listings Sold	0	0	1	0	1	0
Listings Taken	1	0	1	0	0	1
Listing Appts.	4	4	4	4	4	4
Sales	1	1	0	1	0	1
Showing Appts.	8	8	8	8	8	8
Contacts (From 30 Days to $)	400	300	200	200	200	200

Joan's first month activities coincide with the *Up and Running* plan. Joan follows the same contact plan she used for her third month onward to schedule her contacts and business results for the remainder of the year. A planning page similar to this is available for you in Section 12.

FIGURE 2.9   Joan's Plan: From Breakeven to Profitability

1. Estimate your activities and when they will create income. Start with face-to-face contacts.

Activity / Income	1	2	3	4	5	6	7	8	9	10	11	12	Totals
Closings *			1	1		1							
Sales *	1	1		1		1							
Listings sold *					1	1							
Listings secured	1		1		1	1							
Showings	8	8	8	8	8	8							
Listing presentations	4	4	4	4	4	4							
Face-to-face contacts	400	300	200	200	200	200							

Month

*Each unit is worth $3,000 in commissions earned or paid.

2. Tally your expenses per month. Log in your projected earnings and "paids."

	1	2	3	4	5	6	7	8	9	10	11	12	Totals
Business expenses†	1,149	748	818	748	888	818							
Earned income†	3,000	3,000	0	3,000	3,000	6,000							
Paid income	0	0	3,000	3,000	0	3,000							
Profit per month	−$1,149	−$748	$2,182	$2,252	−$888	$2,182							

†See *The Real Estate Agent's Business Planning Guide* for a detailed listing of expenses and budgeting.

FIGURE 2.10 From Breakeven to Profitability

1. Estimate your activities and when they will create income. Start with face-to-face contacts.

Activity / Income	1	2	3	4	5	6	Month 7	8	9	10	11	12	Totals
Closings													
Sales													
Listings sold													
Listings secured													
Showings													
Listing presentations													
Face-to-face contacts													

2. Tally your expenses per month. Log in your projected earnings and "paids."

Business expenses													
Earned income													
Paid income													

Profit per month													

relationship between business-cycle activities, time, expenses, income, and breakeven point—the point where expenses equal income.

If your objectives are similar to Joan Smith, just use her prototype plans for each of the four areas. Each week of her prospecting plan *(30 Days to Dollars)* is in this book, so you can follow it. Also, her whole plan is in one place in Section 11, for your reference. There's also a set of blank planning pages in Section 12 for your use in creating your own plan.

Joan's Breakeven Point.   The sample timeline in Figure 2.9 shows how Joan computed her breakeven and *profit* points. After reading Joan's timeline, complete the blank one in Figure 2.9 to provide you the resources you need to successfully launch your career. The top part of the timeline allows you to fill in business-producing activities. Now, you can see *when* those activities will bring your desired results. The bottom part of the timeline allows you to write in your predicted *business expenses, income* from your sales results and *time* that you will receive this income. (For an in-depth itemization of start-up business expenses, refer to my book, *How about a Career in Real Estate?)*

Adapting Your Plan after the First Month.   After implementing the *30 Days to Dollars* plan for your first 30 days in the business, you will have enough leads to switch to a less aggressive (fewer initial sales calls) prioritized plan. Through tracking successful agents, I have found that agents who stay with the *Up and Running* system break even by month six.

All Your Self-Management Tools

You have just investigated the three tools needed for effective self management:

1. *30 Days to Dollars*—provides a daily prospecting plan and measurement grids to track activities on the sales cycle
2. *Monetary Goals*—plans your one-year goals so you can backtrack to daily activities
3. *From Breakeven to Profitability*—demonstrates how daily activities lead to results; shows how expenses and income create a breakeven point; shows these variables through time (see Figure 2.8)

If your objectives are similar to Joan Smith's, simply use her prototype plans for each of the four areas. For reference, her entire plan is shown in Section 11. A set of blank planning pages for you is in Section 12.

3

Four Weeks to Becoming a Successful Agent

In the previous section, you learned the five principles of successful business management. However, these principles are only a part of what *Up and Running* will do for you. Sections 4 through 7 will provide specific business-producing assignments that will help you cover all the bases as you design your career. At the end of 30 days, you will have accomplished both business-development and business-support goals. Most importantly, you will have mastered the concepts of effective self-management in sales.

By fulfilling the activities to ***develop your business,*** you will:

- have an effective new-agent business plan. You will have the tools to continue this planning process for long-term success.

- with the *30 Days to Dollars* plan, complete a minimum of:

  - 400 proactive prospecting calls

  - 8 qualified appointments to show

  - 1 sale

- 4 listing appointments
- 1 marketable listing
- know exactly how to start and continue the sales cycle.
- have invaluable experience in scheduling your own time to reap results. You will be on your way to effective time management.

By accomplishing the other assignments to support your business, you will:

- create a listing presentation manual.
- design a buyer qualifying/counseling manual.
- complete a listing form.
- carry out a market analysis.
- complete four purchase and sale agreements.
- learn the basics of financing and qualifying.
- observe your office's floor time.
- observe open houses.
- create a contact management system.
- practice the Seven Critical Sales Skills.

Many programs for new agents consist of numerous activities, but few programs show you exactly how to make sales calls. In *Up and Running,* I have included the "how" along with the "what." Sections 8 and 9 contain the critical sales communications skills needed to ensure your success. When you read the weekly assignments, you will see that the how-to's can be referenced from Sections 8 and 9.

Managing Your Program

You manage your program. You are in business for yourself, with your office and manager as support to you. This program is *driven* by you. If you want to capture the support of your manager, meet with him or her weekly. Go over your accomplishments in your business plan. In order to progress faster, get help in your support areas. Each weekly segment contains a checklist for accomplishments with a place for your manager's initials and comments. Use your manager's expertise; you'll get started better and faster.

As a manager, I have come to recognize common success traits in agents. One distinguishing quality is the ability to "demand" a manager's assistance. Inversely, agents who hang back, afraid to ask for the manager's guidance, will be less successful. I really appreciate new agents who consistently make appointments with me to let me know what they are doing, how they are doing it and how I can assist them. That's called *managing the manager!* Obviously, these new agents get much of my attention, concern and positive strokes—the fuel for motivation.

Your goal is to understand and apply effective self-management techniques to create dynamic, professional, long-term business success.

Watch Out Now for Dependent Tendencies

Remember the trends of real estate companies from the "dependent" company, to the independent company, to the inter-dependent company? As you start your real estate career, it's inevitable that you will be feeling insecure of your abilities to sell real estate. All of us have felt that way. It's at this time that you may start feeling that your company owes you something. That something is probably a "lead." Remember, however, leads aren't free. They either cost money in terms of commission splits, or in terms of referral fees. You make the choice. Either you can work an aggressive lead-generating plan like *Up and Running in 30 Days,* or you can sit and wait for leads. When you are wondering if you are starting your business correctly, read this—again.

Successful salespeople always generate their own "leads." Don't fall into a "dependency" mode. You are unwittingly determining that you will never create a powerful business.

Your Business Plan Will Set You Apart in Earning Power

Although successful salespeople generate their own business, the sad truth is that many real estate salespeople aren't very successful. So, as you view the people in your office, be aware that the schedule (they might call it a "business plan") they're following might not be creating much business for them—especially if the schedule they are following is made up only of those activities created by their offices to put them in places where people might find them! In truth, most salespeople rely on office-assigned activities. These include floor time, where they sit and answer the phone about property inquiries—or open houses, where they sit and wait for prospective buyers to appear. So, most salespeople never really create their own business plans. These "salespeople" think that, if the office hires them, they are bound to be successful. Unfortunately, most real estate offices will hire anyone with a license. Being hired has nothing to do with ensuring success; implementing a business start-up plan as described in this program does.

Creating an Independent or an Interdependent Business

Dependent companies are becoming even more so. That is, these companies are promising "leads" to agents for increasingly high prices. These companies also encourage agents to accept these leads, for the companies generate additional income that way. If you're in such a company, must recognize that you will not be able to create a high-producing business through accepting someone else's leads. The reasons are twofold:

1. Accepting someone else's leads doesn't teach you to do relationship marketing; it teaches you to let someone else do the relationships.
2. Having no business plan makes you increasingly reliant on the company and unable to control your own income—you can't stop the company from raising the fees and you can't make the company give you more "leads."

You can work a business start-up plan in a dependent company. You just have to recognize the trends above. To have a personally and professionally dynamic business—a business where the sellers and buyers rely on you over time to serve their real estate needs—be careful that no company takes your "leads" and thereby limits your income.

Note: Some agents are happy to accept leads and pay for them. As long as they recognize that they are not creating their own business, good for them. Just be sure you are creating what you want.

Managing Your Attitude

After you learn the details and process needed to succeed in your plan, you must manage your own plan. The point of this book is to *teach you to manage your plan,* with your manager as "senior partner." Learning these planning concepts and completing these activities is relatively easy. They are, after all, simply a series of tasks. Now, let's add the human being to the process. Plans don't work—people do. As I speak to real estate companies across the United States, managers ask me if this plan works. I tell them: No plan will work unless it's put to work consistently by qualified, dedicated real estate "careerists."

Sounds simple, doesn't it? Just do the work, and you'll be successful. Then why isn't everyone who enters real estate successful?

Behaviors versus Attitudes

Each year many people who enter the real estate field fail to earn the incomes they expected. Many of these agents, disappointed with their incomes, leave the business within the first year. Some stay in the business, not earning what they expected but subsidized by other incomes or spouses.

One reason for this contrast between goals and reality is that agents start the real estate business without a clear idea of their job description. They do not realize what new agents must do to be successful. They may think that showing up at the office five days a week to "take floor time" guarantees a paycheck! They do not realize that their success depends on *frequently* starting and continuing the business cycle that is discussed in this book. Then, after new agents have been in the business a few weeks, they discover that *their* job description does not bring the anticipated income. They find that a successful agent's job description is different from theirs (see Figure 3.1). Their enthusiasm about the business wanes. In effect, their *attitude* about the business changes. I call these agents *no-start failures.* They did not have a chance to succeed in the business because they did not enter the business with an understanding of what was required to succeed. If agents do not understand the job, they cannot commit to the work.

A tip for managers: Show *Up and Running* to your prospective agents during the interview process. Ask them to read the book and project themselves performing these activities. Ask them if they will commit to doing this work—in the amount of time required and the numbers needed for success. Interviewees will appreciate your honest assessment of the behaviors and commitment levels required for success in today's real estate world. The net result will be that you'll hire winners.

How Our Attitudes Change with the Challenge

With *Up and Running,* you have a clear idea of what successful agents do to launch a career. You have committed to this plan—this job description. End of discussion, right? Wrong. All of us have our "ups and downs" as we struggle through anything new. Change is difficult.

As a new agent, you start the business with:

- enthusiasm,
- confidence,
- high self-esteem, and
- excitement.

FIGURE 3.1   A Successful Agent's Job Description

A successful agent consistently performs four categories of activities:

1. Business-developing plan
   - Find potential customers and clients by identifying target markets. Then, identify particular personal strengths. Create programs using strengths to reach these particular markets. Execute these programs daily.

   - Sample target markets
     - People you already know socially
     - People you know from former business
     - People you know from church/sports/organizations
     - People in your neighborhood/chosen neighborhood
     - People you meet in promoting seller's home

   Our agent's income and success is determined by the number of people contacted consistently in these target markets.

2. Sales activities generated as result of business-developing plan
   - Showing homes to qualified customers
   - Selling homes
   - Listing marketable properties to sell in normal market time

3. Activities that guarantee a check
   - Selling homes
   - Your listings sell

4. Preparation and support activities that supplement the business-producing activities
   - Preview properties
   - Paperwork/sales follow-up
   - Education
   - Meetings

By working an aggressive, personally tailored business plan, the successful agent ensures early income and long-term success,

You tell your manager that you're tenacious, that you can handle rejection. The manager need not worry that you'll do the activities because you're a self-starter and can motivate yourself. Then you start performing the activities. You've always thought of yourself as a good communicator. However, as you prospect, you find it difficult to communicate. People somehow create many ways to reject you. You've always liked people, and you sense they like you. Yet they act differently with you now that you're in sales. People make up stories to avoid you, say they "have a friend in the business," secure information from you but do not give you information, promise to meet with you at the office—but don't show up. You experience feelings of:

- rejection,
- frustration,
- impatience,
- self-doubt, and
- inadequacy.

Your image of yourself is tested. Who is the real *you?* The one who feels confident and tenacious and is a self-starter? Or the one who feels rejected, frustrated, inadequate, and full of self-doubt? Your attitude about the business—and yourself—is in danger of shifting from *positive* to *negative.*

Attitudes Can Change in Seconds.   Each day, hour, and minute, you evaluate your feelings about the business. Your *experiences* as you perform the activities in this plan fuel this evaluation. Your *conclusions* are based on your personal belief system. It's not the activities that cause you to have a certain attitude about the business, but the conclusions you draw from your experiences with these activities. Let's say you have knocked on 50 doors without getting a lead. What do you conclude? Agents who will fail conclude that "this won't work in this area." Agents who will succeed imagine themselves one step closer to a lead with every rejection. These agents realize that they must experience many rejections to get success.

Managing Attitude Shifts.   Managers can teach new agents what activities to do, how to do them, and how to monitor them to evaluate effectiveness. Using the forms provided in this book, managers and agents can track agents' actual *behaviors* each day. But who will keep track of changing attitudes? Who will manage the conclusions about these activities? These emotional evaluations flit through a new agent's head hundreds of times a day. *How* these constantly changing attitudes are managed determines whether or not the agent will succeed.

What Agents Want.   According to a recent survey of real estate salespeople, one of the most important services agents want from their manager is to *provide positive* motivation. Sounds easy, doesn't it? Part of it is. It's not difficult to create a positive atmosphere in the office. It is difficult to find out what motivates each individual (everyone has different motivators). And it is more difficult to design a motivational program to fit each agent's need-time in the business, motivators, outside influences, etc. Moreover, it's *very* difficult for a manager to manage the constant flux of attitudes, to catch agents when they are falling into depression and to pump them up. Agents' attitudes change hundreds of times a day. When agents get down, they usually talk to themselves—negatively. How can managers manage agents' ups and downs? They can't—but they can *teach* new agents how to manage their ups and downs.

Becoming a Managing Master of Your Attitudes.   Managing your attitude requires three steps:

1. *Recognize your attitude* will change about the business as you do the activities in the business.
2. *Acknowledge* each time you draw a conclusion about your activities.
3. *Develop a process* for controlling your conclusions.

Evaluating Your Attitudinal Process.   To evaluate and manage your attitude, try this simple, effective method. In a notebook, divide each page into six columns:

- Self-talk

- Conclusions of your self-talk

- Positive attitude

- Negative attitude

- Revised conclusion/revised attitude

- Belief

As you go about your business day, keep the notebook handy. Write down each time you talk to yourself—positively and negatively. Let's say you just held an open house. As you are leaving, you say to yourself: "What's wrong with me? I thought I was a good communicator, but these people coming into my open house won't tell me anything."

Write down the conclusion you drew: *Maybe I'm not cut out for this business." Note* these thoughts in the proper column—*positive* or *negative.* Obviously, the above comment and conclusion would go in the negative column.

Managing Your Conclusions for a Positive Attitude.   Studies show that most self-talk is *negative,* which naturally leads to a *negative* conclusion. People will talk to themselves about this conclusion 10 to 20 times and convince themselves that this conclusion is true! Thus, when agents conclude that they cannot be successful in open houses, that idea plays again and again in their minds until they change their positive attitude about their success in the business—and form a new belief about their ability to communicate.

You can stop this insidious—although natural—process by replacing it with a new process. To do this, you must replace your natural inclination of *negative* self-talk, repeated again and again, with *some positive* self-talk, repeated again and again.

Retraining Your Mind.   Is this the conclusion about open houses that you really want to draw? Is this the attitude that will ensure your success in this business? Can you change your conclusion and attitude? Tough-minded, success-oriented people can adjust their conclusions and attitudes about their experiences to reach their goals. They experience the same rejection, self-doubt, frustration, and anxieties that failure-oriented people do. The only difference is that these tough-minded people have developed a mental system to reinterpret their conclusions. It's as simple as substituting a different conclusion, along with a change in attitude. So, go back to your notebook and write a new conclusion to your experience. For the example above, it might be: *Based on my results, I'm not as good a communicator as I thought I was. I need to improve my communication skills. I can get these skills by taking a sales skill course, by observing agents who are successful at open houses, and by practicing my new skills.*

Making Your New Conclusion Believable.   The last column in your notebook, *belief,* is very important. If you don't *believe* that you can create a new conclusion, you will not take the action steps. In the *belief* column, add a statement that backs up your opinion about skills enhancement. It might be: *I know that, if other agents can be successful getting appointments at open houses, I can be, too. It's just a matter of my learning, practicing, and perfecting the skills required.*

Being Tough-Minded Enough to Succeed. The ability to *consciously* control your attitude is a skill that can be learned. To ensure your success in real estate, assume that you need to develop tough-mindedness. By following the steps outlined, you can become tough-minded enough to succeed in real estate.

There are many excellent self-help books on how to create a positive mental attitude, as well as courses and videos on self-esteem. One of the best courses, developed by Lou Tice, is offered at his Pacific Institute in Seattle, Washington.

Controlling your attitude is simple if you recognize that it's a *skill* that can be learned. It takes practice, tenacity, and patience. But isn't it worth it if it ensures your success in real estate? You have a proven, successful, activity-based, business-developing program in *Up and Running*. You have a manager committed to your success. You have the tools to retrain your mind and control your attitude. You are set for success!

The Manager's Role

It's tough out there. Agents enter the real estate business with enthusiasm, hope, and determination. Then they find out what rejection means, and their enthusiasm quickly withers under the stress of starting anew.

Managers can help. This book offers new agents (and those attempting to re-jump-start their careers) a program that will ensure a successful career. However, to start and continue a challenging program (whether it's a diet or a new job), every agent needs encouragement—not just "atta boy, keep going" kind of support but *real, specific, constructive guidance and feedback* that will help the agent to build a successful daily plan and to know that it is working.

How Managers Can Help Agents and Still Have Time to Run the Office

In their quest to make a profit, managers must do everything from counsel agents to run the administrative part of the office. It's difficult for managers to provide new agents the guidance needed to get their careers off to a quick, successful start. *Up and Running* relieves managers' concerns because it provides the plan and resources new agents need to begin a successful career.

Up and Running is based on the assumption that new agents are truly in business for themselves—with their managers as *consultants*. Agents are responsible for completing each weekly assignment. Managers meet with the agent weekly (the agent sets the appointment) to review the agent's accomplishments and to add information specific to the office and market area. The grids entitled "Accomplishments" in Sections 4 through 7 provide managers and agents an opportunity to review the areas completed each week.

Managers are committed to the success of each new agent hired. *Up and Running* gives managers the foundation to build a business relationship that agents will appreciate throughout their entire careers.

Manager-Agent "Success" Agreement

As in any successful partnership, the new agent has the best chance to succeed when the agent and manager work closely together. To ensure that manager and agent are sharing mutual expectations, use the Agreement To Ensure That You're *Up and Running* (see Figure 3.2).

> *Note to managers: With all the tasks we have to achieve, providing the time and support necessary to ensure a new agent's fast start is difficult. For the past ten years, I have developed another support system to work in tandem with* Up and Running. *It's called* "Crosscoaching": A Proven Mentor Program. *(See References for details.)*

Should You Find a Coach?

Independent coaching around the country has become a trend in all businesses over the last few years. Although training is important, too often the concepts and skills introduced in training are left in the training room. Coaching fills the gap between the training room and "on your own" real life. A good in-office coach can do the following:

1. Hold you accountable to the goals you say you want to accomplish
2. Let you "shadow" the coach as the coach goes about sales activities, such as prospecting, listing presentations, selling presentations, and negotiating
3. Share "how-to's" and packaging (such as listing packages)

Don't expect a coach to be an "answer man", however. Moreover, don't expect a coach to coach you without your having a specific "game plan"—such as the *Up and Running* start-up plan.

If coaching programs fail, it's usually because of three reasons:

1. The coach and agent had different expectations of each other. The contract needs to spell out exactly what is expected of each party.
2. The coach and agent didn't agree upon a game plan. If you want a coach, be prepared to get into action fast, so the coach has

---

FIGURE 3.2 Agreement to Ensure That You're *Up and Running*

I, _____, agree to complete all the assignments in *Up and Running in 30 Days* because I intend to design a career to be successful quickly and professionally.

I want support from my manager, so I agree to make an appointment with my manager weekly. During that appointment, I will review my work for that week and my plan for the next week.

I understand that doing the work according to the priorities and numbers in *Up and Running in 30 Days* is the professional's method of beginning my business.

To ensure that I get the most from my work, I expect my manager to:

* meet with me weekly for at least one-half hour;
* help me keep my activities prioritized correctly;
* provide assistance in my development of specific business methods;
* provide me any resources necessary to complete the assignments; and
* provide the support and encouragement necessary to begin a successful career.

I understand it's my business, and I agree to manage it according to the principles in *Up and Running in 30 Days* because I want to create a successful, high-producing, professional career.

Agent _____   Manager _____

Date of this agreement: _____ End of program: _____

---

something to coach you to! Don't expect your coach to motivate you to do the activities you know you should do—but won't!

3. The coach wasn't trained. Before you sign up with a coach, see the whole coaching program—in writing—to ensure it's really a program, not just an after-thought.

Up and Running: An Overview of Your Four Weeks

Each week, for four weeks, you will complete the following activities:

1. *Create your weekly and daily plan.* Use the provided planners; refer back to the Prototype Schedule and *30 Days to Dollars* plan. Be sure to keep a balance of business-producing activities and support activities. Ask your manager to assess the balance of your plan. Creating your plan and assessing it, two of the most valuable self-management tools in *Up and Running,* provide the basis for making good business judgments throughout your entire career.

2. *Use the* **30 Days to Dollars** *plan and grid.* The business activity plan is provided to you each week, so you can easily plan your activities and track results.

3. *Track business-producing activities.* For each day and for the week, a grid is provided to help you track your results. This way, you will create your own *ratios of success,* so that you can analyze and make adjustments to your business in the future.

4. *Practice and apply new sales skills.* To optimize your contact with potential buyers and sellers, *Up and Running* provides the critical sales skills you need to save time and to convert more prospects to real buyers and sellers.

5. *Complete business support activities.* You need confidence in your ability to make sales calls. These business-supporting activities provide the confidence you need to create a top-producing business.

6. *Meet with your manager for support, information, and encouragement.* It's difficult to "go it alone," and your manager is committed to your success. *Up and Running* provides a solid foundation for communication between you and your manager.

Turning Contacts into Real Buyers and Sellers

Besides the business-managing and weekly assignments in *Up and Running,* there are two other critical parts to this system to ensure that you get results from your sales efforts:

1. The Seven Critical Sales Skills
2. Qualifying Buyers and Sellers

Seven Critical Sales Skills

In this four-week plan, you will develop valuable sales skills. A foundation of *Up and Running,* these sales skills are introduced and explained in Section 9. Each week you will practice and apply new skills, developing them in four ways:

1. Reading the synopsis of the prospecting methods/scripts in the appendix
2. Interviewing agents
3. Practicing these skills with a fellow professional
4. Practicing these skills in the field

Your sales skills form the basis to begin your sales career. Use them, adapt them, apply them to all situations that require effective communication skills.

Sales Skills—"Specialty" Communication

Do you consider yourself a good communicator? Most people who enter real estate think one of their biggest strengths is their ability to communicate. When I mention communicate, what do you think of? To many of us, to communicate means to *talk.* If we're good talkers, we assume we would be good salespeople. When we enter real estate, we take courses in finance, escrow, title insurance, and building inspections in order to *talk to strangers (potential customers and clients) with authority.* After all, if anyone asked us a question, we would be embarrassed if we didn't know the answer—and we start talking our way right out of a real estate career!

Why? Because people don't care how much you *know* until they know how much you *care.* How do you show that you care about others? Ask them questions; listen to them. People want to be *listened to, understood,* and *empathized with.* Instead of learning facts and figures to dazzle prospects, the most important communication skill to hone is *listening.*

To become a good listener, practice the following skills that effective listeners have developed:

- Listen for inflections, pauses, the pace—the "music" of the talk rather than the "words."
- Actively acknowledge the talker (e.g., "yes, okay, hmm").
- Repeat what the talker said to be sure you correctly understood it.
- Ask for more clarification of what the talker said.
- Avoid jumping to conclusions and talking.

Are You a Good Listener?   Generally, people assume that they're good listeners. But, in truth, most people just listen carefully enough to get the gist and long enough to get ready to talk! They're thinking about what they're going to say rather than listening effectively. Recently, I was teaching a large group of managers how to apply counseling techniques for use with their agents. One principle of counseling is that, to solve the problem, we must get to the *root* of the problem. Often the agent's problem isn't really a problem but a symptom. During the class, I showed managers a proven counseling process that worked. Then I asked the managers to use this process, which required them to demonstrate all the listening skills in the class. Although they resisted taking the time to probe, listen, and clarify, the managers acknowledged that the process worked. Following the process, they restrained from offering a pat solution and, as they probed further, discovered that the problem was different from what they had first assumed. Their initial solution, had they offered it, would have been wrong.

The same holds true for you with your customers and clients. They have problems, objections, beliefs. You must take the time to find out exactly what is on your customers' minds and in their hearts to help them meet their needs. *Effective listening is the most important communication skill to develop for a successful real estate career.*

What Do Sales Skills Have To Do with Listening?   I hope that I have convinced you that listening is the most important communication skill to develop for success in sales. But how can you listen if people won't talk to you? You hold an open house, but people avoid you. You get a call on an ad, but the caller doesn't offer any information. How do you "prime the pump"—get people to talk to you—so that you can listen?

Learn To Ask Questions—The Right Questions.   When I was a child, my aunts would chide my mother because she always took the time to answer my questions—my *hundreds* of questions! My aunts thought my mother gave me too much detail, too much attention, too much time. But I learned so much because my mother treated my questions with respect. I learned that you learn by asking questions, not by talking. I learned that, when I got my mom to talk, she forgot to ask *me* any questions—like, had I practiced the piano that day. As long as I kept her talking, I controlled the conversation!

Control the Conversation.   Let's go back to the open house scenario. The prospects come in. Their objective is to get information from you while keeping secret any information about themselves. They know the principle of controlling conversations. Being effective communicators, they ask, "What's the price of this home?" Ready to prove that you are a knowledgeable real estate agent, you relate the price, the terms, the insulation value, the prices in the neighborhood and so on. You're really communicating—you think. The prospects thank you and walk out. You kick yourself. You didn't get an appointment.

What went wrong? You proved that you were knowledgeable. Why didn't the prospects volunteer information—give you their names, social security numbers, and undying loyalty? Because you didn't ask. They got the information they wanted and controlled the conversation; you got nothing. This is not effective communication. Yet I have observed this scenario dozens of times. With effective listening and questioning skills, you could remedy this situation.

Listening and questioning skills are right here—in a sales format. The Seven Critical Sales Skills—see Section 9—are designed to put you in control—to help you ask the right questions and really listen to your potential customers and clients. These are simply effective communication skills adapted to a sales format.

Applying Relationship Skills.   At the beginning of the sales process, you aren't looking for "closes". That is, you don't want to be manipulating the sellers' and buyers' answers so that they agree with you. That's an old-style selling technique. Instead, you want to ask sincere questions to establish an enduring relationship, to establish trust and confidence in your abilities. Great relationships are the basis of referral business. Think of it this way: It's better to get three referrals from a person than to sell that person one home. Keep in mind that you are starting a relationship that should endure for years.

Refining Your Communication Skills.   Few agents, including experienced salespeople and managers, are as skilled at listening and questioning as they could be. To refine your communication abilities, practice listening and questioning skills until you:

- *really* understand customers' and clients' needs;
- can define *exactly* what customers mean when they say they want *a deal* (each customer has a different definition);
- are *listening* two-thirds of the time you're with a customer, and *talking* one-third of the time;
- secure at least one solid appointment per open house;

- get most of the people at your open house to share their real estate needs with you;
- obtain the names and phone numbers, along with appointments, if they qualify, of three-quarters of the people who call you during your floor time;
- can discover the dominant buying motive (motivation) of each buyer and seller you work with—in your first interview; and
- can consistently remove barriers and communicate effectively with buyers and sellers to get them the homes they want—and want to sell.

Qualifying Buyers and Sellers

According to new agents, the most difficult challenge to master is time management. For many, problems with time management stem from an inability to control buyers and sellers. To get you off on the right foot and help you spend your time effectively, use the following four sales resources to qualify your buyers and sellers.

For buyers:

1. Qualified buyer checklist
2. Buyer log

For sellers:

3. Seller log
4. Marketable listing checklist

As you qualify buyers and sellers each week, log them in on the grids (see Section 10). Be sure the buyers and sellers meet the standards you set.

Before you set a buyer or seller appointment, ask yourself if the buyer or seller meets the standards set on these grids. After the appointment, go back to the grid and requalify your prospect. Instead of working with poorly qualified buyers and sellers—as many new agents do—simply go back into the field and find more prospects. Take the attitude that your prospect is *lucky* to be working with you!

Developing Your Qualifying Skills.   There are quite a number of ways to develop your qualifying skills. Among them are the following.

Listening, Questioning, Qualifying.   To review the value of communication skills, listening makes the difference in an agent's career success. However, an agent can't listen to buyers or sellers if they don't talk. To encourage customers and clients to talk, the most effective method is to ask questions. Although this pattern of asking questions to get the other person to talk may seem obvious, it is not our normal social pattern.

Evaluating Social Conversations. Tomorrow, listen to three social conversations. How do the people proceed? How many questions does each person ask of the other? How many follow-up questions are asked? Does the person asking the question get impatient and want to talk? Does this person look anxious to give an answer? This is normal social habit: Communication means making statements and expecting the other person to listen.

Sales Communication Is Different. In sales, this social exchange method of communication just doesn't work when you need information from the prospect to start and continue the sales cycle. To discover the prospect's reasons for purchasing, desires or motivations, you must consistently ask questions and listen. You must talk one-third of the time and listen two-thirds. What a difference! It takes time to change social communication habits to sales communication habits. However, agents who *never* learn to change their patterns are not very successful.

Develop Qualifying Questions. The grids in *Up and Running* for qualifying buyers and sellers (see Section 9) are used by successful, experienced agents. Use these grids to develop qualifying questions to use in the interview process for buyers and sellers. First, let's look at the grids for sellers.

Qualifying Sellers: A Priority. Following is a common scenario for new agents (even some experienced agents still fall into this trap): A prospective client calls during your floor time and requests a market analysis on his home. You're so excited that you make an appointment without asking any qualifying questions. You inspect the home and do all the work required to complete a market analysis. You return to the home and give the prospective client your complete, full-color, 20-page market analysis. You don't hear from him. You call and find out that he wanted the market analysis to give to his niece, who just entered the real estate field, for an assignment in her training school. You feel used. However, the prospective client feels that, because you provided the market analysis service without qualifying him, he got what he wanted. And he assumes that you got what you wanted. *Was* it what you wanted?

Setting Qualifying Standards for Your Level of Professionalism. To avoid feeling used, act like a pro. Take doctors, for example. When you go into a doctor's office for the first time, you fill out a form (the doctor is qualifying you). If you don't answer questions on the form, the nurse gives the form back to get the answers to those questions—or you don't get to see the doctor!

Qualifying the Seller at the Beginning of the Process.   Generally, to list a property, agents use a two-step process:

1. *Qualify* the seller and the property for salability.
2. *Present* your marketing plan, including pricing, to the seller.

Qualifying starts in the first phone conversation with the seller. The agent needs to find out:

- what the seller wants, and
- why the seller wants it.

Looking at the grid (see Figure 3.3), what questions would you need to ask over the phone to decide whether you want to visit a prospective client's home? Jot down these questions. Then, query three top agents in your office about the questions they ask—and the answers they look for—before they make an appointment to begin the listing process. For example, if you ask the seller why he or she wants a market analysis and the reply is, "For insurance purposes," what would you do?

Qualifying continues when the agent visits the seller and inspects the property. During the first appointment, the agent's goal is to ascertain whether the seller wants to list the property.

Think of it this way. It's much like the doctor who asks qualifying questions rather than jumps to conclusions. Jumping to conclusions could mean a wrong diagnosis—and a wrong treatment. To be successful in real estate, agents should take the same approach. Ask sellers lots of questions about themselves—you are qualifying them. What are some things you would want to know about a seller before committing to do a marketing plan? In other words, what are some qualifying questions? (For example, two important questions are: When do you want to move? Where are you moving?)

After you've outlined some qualifying questions, query three listing agents in your office about the questions they ask sellers to qualify them prior to "diagnosing treatment" and creating a marketing plan.

Gathering Information.   Many agents think that their job during the first visit is to gather information about the home. They do not realize that it's more important to their career to qualify the seller than to inspect the home! So, they focus on the number of bathrooms and bedrooms

FIGURE 3.3 **For Sellers: Qualified Listing Appointments**

Date of Presentation	Name	Address	Want To Sell Both Home	2 Hours Pre-Scheduled	How Much $ Want	Marketing Presentation Completed	Results

and forget that the seller's motivation, loyalty, and needs must be understood and met. This is the information that forms the basis for your marketing plan.

Establishing Professional Boundaries.   You have qualified the seller over the phone, inspected the property and asked the seller numerous questions. Next, you complete the research on the property and prepare the marketing plan (including the pricing analysis). Now, you're ready to present your marketing plan to the seller.

Pause a minute. Before you make the second appointment with the seller, consider what would cause you *not* to make that second appointment. What professional boundaries have you established to ensure that you do not waste your time with unmotivated sellers and unmarketable properties?

What Happens When Agents Have Established Boundaries?   Let's look at an agent who's made a tough, professional personal boundary of not listing properties she has determined will not sell in normal market time. This agent will not list properties that are more than three percent over her analysis of what that property will actually sell for. Why this personal boundary? This "pro" wants to establish a name for herself as a REALTOR® who only lists properties that sell. Her reputation depends on "sold" signs on properties. Obviously, this reputation will attract only serious sellers, who appreciate her professional attitude. During the first appointment, if she determines that the sellers want more money for their home than her initial professional opinion indicates, she will not make the next appointment. Why should she waste her time and ruin her reputation? Or, if, after the second appointment, the sellers want more money for their home than her expert opinion warrants, she won't list the home.

Recently, I saw how this strategy works. An agent in my office prepared a marketing plan for a seller. However, because the competition priced the property $50,000 higher than our agent, the seller chose to list with the competition. Unfortunately, the competition did not work in our area and used the wrong homes to diagnose the home's selling challenges.

The seller, initially, was pleased with the listing agent because he listed the home at such a high price. Of course, the seller expected selling agents to bring customers. However, agents who wanted to create trust and loyalty with their buyers would not show the overpriced home to their buyers. So the seller saw few potential buyers.

After three months of lost marketing time, the disillusioned seller listed with our agent at the right price. However, irreparable damage had been done to all parties involved. National surveys show that this added time on market will cost the seller thousands of dollars. Homes that are on the market a long time sell for less than if they were listed at the right price and sold quickly. (Remember Charles Revson's marketing truism: Create demand. When buyers compete, the price goes up.) Because the first listing agent did not create a satisfied customer, he or she will not get any return business. Unfortunately, the agent who lists the home the second time around won't have as satisfied a customer as if he had been able to list the home first—at the right price. In conclusion, over-pricing properties brings negative results to sellers, listing agents and selling agents.

Evaluate Property Salability.   Sellers qualify agents. And good agents carefully qualify sellers. How confident would you feel if your doctor did not ask you any questions but simply prescribed aspirin every time you came to the office?

Sellers' confidence in an agent is raised when they know that the agent has established certain criteria for marketing property. Why waste sellers' time—and money—if the property won't sell? Look at the salability checklist in Figure 3.4. What questions for the first and second visits would provide information to help you decide whether or not to list this property? What questions and criteria would you add for your own professional boundaries? How could you use this list with sellers?

Determine your bottom-line objective with sellers? Is it to list property? To post signs? To sell as many of your listings as possible? Perhaps it is to list only properties that will sell in normal market time or to create high levels of customer satisfaction to get lots of referral business. Do you want to create an image for yourself as a real estate agent whose properties always sell quickly? Establish your boundaries based on your desired levels of professionalism. You decide—it's your career.

Qualifying Buyers: A New Approach.   With the changes in agency representation, you will consider working with buyers exactly as you have always worked with sellers. Qualify and list buyers to work with you throughout the entire process of purchasing a home. This means that, when you first meet a buyer, begin the qualifying process. For example, as you are holding open house, you meet a potential buyer. Some questions you need to ask are:

- How long have you been looking for a home?
- When do you want/need to move?
- Have you been prequalified by a lender?

FIGURE 3.4   Evaluate Property Salability

1. Property listed at competitive price.   Yes_____   No_____

2. Full-term listing agreement.   Yes_____   No_____

3. Seller to complete obvious repairs/cleaning prior to showing.   Yes_____   No_____

4. Easy access (e.g., key, phone for showing).   Yes_____   No_____

5. Yard sign.   Yes_____   No_____

6. Immediate possession.   Yes_____   No_____

7. Extras included (e.g., appliances)   Yes_____   No_____

8. Available for first tour.   Yes_____   No_____

9. Government terms available.   Yes_____   No_____

10. Owner financing available.   Yes_____   No_____

11. Below market down payment.   Yes_____   No_____

12. Below market interest rate.   Yes_____   No_____

13. Post-dated price reduction.   Yes_____   No_____

14. Market commission.   Yes_____   No_____

15. In my evaluation, this property will sell within listed market range, in normal market time for this area.   Yes_____   No_____

16. My credibility as a professional will be enhanced by listing this property   Yes_____   No_____

What questions would you ask before you decide to make an appointment to show the buyer homes? Refine your professional boundaries. Would you show a buyer homes without knowing the answers to several key questions? To discover other key questions, ask three agents in your office what preliminary qualifying questions help them to qualify a buyer. Ask them their professional boundaries.

The Qualifying or Consulting Session.   To avoid making a poor buying decision, today's buyers need a lot of information *before* they look at homes. Buyers need a way to get this information from someone they can trust. Here's where you come in. Develop a method to meet with and consult with potential buyers *before* they begin looking at properties. Develop informational materials. At the same time, wrap into this informational system a qualifying questionnaire. You will not only provide information to buyers, you will qualify them in a professional manner. You are choosing the buyer as the buyer is selecting you.

A System To Assist You.   Because listing buyers is a new concept, I have developed a system for you to use to inform and quality buyers. This system/method, similar to the listing systems for sellers you use through your company, is called *The Complete Buyer's Agent Kit* and consists of a 24-page booklet for buyers, which explains the purchasing process and your value in this process. A 2-page questionnaire with the critical questions you need to ask buyers is included. Most questionnaires for buyers focus on their physical needs in a home (e.g., number of bedrooms, baths). Unfortunately, the buyers' real needs, their emotional needs, are not addressed. The questionnaire developed in *The Complete Buyer's Agent Kit* assists the buyer and agent in pinpointing the root of the concern, so that the agent can pick the right homes to show the buyer. In addition to the booklet for buyers, there is a confidential separate section for agents on how to create added value and credibility, and how to earn respect for your services. There's also information on how to create loyalty during the sale—and after. The agents' main concerns when working with buyers are to create value-added services that set them apart from the average "licensee"—so the buyer will have reasons to choose them exclusively.

The Guide for Qualifying Buyers.   Now, let's look at how the following grids can assist you as you develop qualifying questions and professional boundaries for working with buyers.

The first grid (see Figure 3.5) helps you to keep track of your appointments. Note the "both at qualifying session" column. We have

FIGURE 3.5   Qualified Buyers

Log a record of your appointments throughout the program.

Date of Qualify Meeting	Name	Address	Qualify Checklist Used	Both @ Qualifying Session	# Showings	Sales

learned that showing homes to only one person when two are buying is an exercise in futility. You need to get to know both parties, for their motivations may be entirely different from one another. I recommend that you draw a professional boundary at showing homes to one party over a period of time without the other.

Note the "number of showings" column in Figure 3.5. (This is important data to keep.) The rule of thumb says that you must put people (not the same people) in your car eight times to sell a home. Let's say your goal is to sell one home per month. How many times per week, on average, must you put people in your car? Right. Twice. However, because you're new at this game, your conversion ratios may be different. Keep track, and, if necessary, adjust your numbers to reach your goals.

What the Conversion Ratios Will Tell You. Considering that the agent's greatest concern is time management, think of the time wasted if agents put people in their cars and showed them homes without qualifying them! Yet, agents frequently do this. Janis, an experienced agent, had shown homes 25 times in the last few weeks, yet had made no sales. She was frustrated because she had been working so hard with no results. What was wrong? Perhaps she wasn't qualifying buyers or showing the wrong homes. If she had used a good qualifying questionnaire and learned to ask questions and to listen, she would have shown the right homes. Perhaps she wasn't closing. Again, if Janis had used a good qualifying questionnaire, she would have known the buyers' motivation—and could have helped the buyers make a buying decision at the right time. Successful results depend on a well-crafted, well-practiced, well-organized consulting/qualifying meeting.

As you read the criteria for evaluating your customer's potential (see Figure 3.6), qualifying questions will become obvious. Jot these questions down. Ask three agents in your office about their qualifying questions. Ask about their professional boundaries. What will yours be? When I was a new agent, no one told me to qualify buyers. I just put everyone who wanted to look at homes in my car. I saw lots of homes, but I sure got tired! Finally, I developed a qualifying process. Guess what? Buyers respected me, they complied with my requests and they met my standards. Why? Because I had created something of value—something other agents did not provide. In my *List the Buyer System* (see References), I have listed dozens of services that I provided to loyal buyers—and you can provide—to build value.

Establishing a Value-Added Service Approach. Studies show that buyers think that the greatest service a REALTOR® provides is showing

FIGURE 3.6   Evaluate Your Customer's Potential

Rate on a scale of 1–4 (4 is the highest)

1. Customer is motivated to purchase.
   (Rate each spouse/partner separately.)   1   2   3   4

2. Customer is realistic about price range expectations.   1   2   3   4

3. Customer is open and cooperative.   1   2   3   4

4. Customer will purchase in a timely manner.   1   2   3   4

5. Customer is a referral source and will provide referrals.   1   2   3   4

6. Customer has agreed that you will be his or her
   exclusive agent.   1   2   3   4

7. Agent has established a positive rapport with customer.   1   2   3   4

8. Customer will meet with loan officer.   1   2   3   4

9. Customer answered financial questions openly.   1   2   3   4

10. Customer has no other agent obligations.   1   2   3   4

11. If customer has home to sell, he or she is realistic
    about price.   1   2   3   4

12. Customer will devote sufficient time to purchasing
    process.   1   2   3   4

13. Both spouses/partners will be available to look for home.   1   2   3   4

Is this customer worthy of your time, energy, and expertise?

listed homes! If that were true, they could choose any agent. But you and I know that the services agents provide are wide and varied. Some agents don't even call prospects back! Some agents have other jobs and work only part-time in the profession. Other agents don't update their knowledge and skills, so they can't help buyers with new information. The list goes on and on.

To create buyer loyalty, establish your own list of value-added services. Where will your level of professionalism be? After establishing your list, decide how to communicate these services to buyers early in the building-rapport stage. With your professional stance and your ability to communicate, you have started the listing-the-buyer process, which will be a win-win for both buyer and agent.

When does a new agent get tough about qualifying? Perhaps you're thinking: If I qualify sellers and buyers, I won't have nearly as many listings as lots of agents I know. I won't be putting as many people in my car. I'm not sure I'm ready to be tough—yet. Okay. *When* and *how* will you get tougher?

Many agents think that they will "get tough later." Bob (not his real name), an agent in my office, refused to qualify buyers. He simply tried to talk to them between showing homes, while driving them around. He said that he would qualify them better when he was more successful. Bob lasted in the business only a few months. He felt people took advantage of him. He had trouble closing; he thought that closing techniques would solve his buyer problems. In truth, though, closing techniques are inconsequential when compared to a great qualifying system. In today's world of sophisticated buyers, qualifying systems with prioritized information are the key to sales success.

More Prospecting Solves the "Tough" Dilemma.   *Don't do what I did*—wasting your time hauling unqualified non-prospects around is not fun or productive. Start right—prospect for hundreds of potentially qualified prospects. Be tough when you qualify them. You will be able to list only qualified properties because you will have too many potential listings to spend time with uncooperative sellers and overpriced listings.

Managers are not impressed with busy work; they are impressed with *results.* A listing isn't a result; a *sold* listing is a result. Be kind to yourself. Start the business with a careerist approach. Develop professional standards and boundaries. Treat yourself with respect, and buyers and sellers will respect you. Using the four qualifying grids automatically boosts your professionalism. Here's to great qualifying!

4

Week One

You are now familiar with the concepts of successful business development. You have some insights about managing your attitude. You understand the numbers involved in planning your business. You are ready to translate all this knowledge into action. In Sections 4 through 7, I have provided a detailed, precise weekly action plan to ensure your success. In each week's plan, you'll first see the objectives—your short-term goals for the week. To keep your priorities correct, these objectives are divided between *business development* and *business support.* In each group, your weekly activities are outlined. Along with accomplishing your sales goals, you will be gaining sales skills. At the end of each week, you will tally your accomplishments to share with your manager. Dive in now—start creating your picture of success!

Objectives

Business Development

- Begin *30 Days to Dollars* with the best sources of prospects—people you know.
- Make 100 sales calls.
- Get two qualified buyer leads.
- Get two qualified seller leads.
- Show homes to two qualified buyer groups.
- Go to at least one listing appointment.
- Apply three new sales skills in sales situations.

Business Support

- Create a workable weekly plan based on good business principles. Translate this plan to a daily plan.
- Develop a working knowledge of the listing agreement and the information sources for that agreement.
- Develop a working knowledge of market analysis. Learn how to package a market analysis. Learn three methods of countering sellers' objections to pricing.
- Practice three new sales skills.
- Begin compiling your contact management database.

Preparation for Reactive Activities

- Understand how public open houses draw potential customers and clients.
- Develop a working knowledge of the floor time system in your office—if floor time is available to you.

Note: Reactive activities will not be discussed again in further sections. See your office training program for specific training in open houses and floor time.

Weekly Activity Plan

Using the weekly planner in Figure 4.1, plan your first week. Create your plan in the following order:

1. Log in office-scheduled events (e.g., office meeting, tour).
2. Log in assignments from office (e.g., floor time, open house).
3. Log is meeting with the manager.
4. Log in business-producing activities/those on business cycle (e.g., showings, listing presentations, writing offers).
5. Log in business-development activities.
6. Log in support activities, including inspecting inventory and support assignments given here.

See Figure 4.2, *Joan's Weekly Plan—First Week,* as an example of a completed weekly planner. Note: You may choose to enter your schedule into a personal digital assistant (PDA) or a pocket personal computer (PC). This will allow you to view your schedule at any time, along with your contacts and other pertinent information.

Your Daily Plan

Now, prioritize your activities for the week, placing them in your daily planner, shown in Figure 4.3. (Six daily plans are included for the four weeks covered in Sections 4 through 7.) Use your daily planner to log in your sales accomplishments.

Business Development

Using the *30 Days to Dollars* format discussed in Section 2, start prospecting. Begin with people you know. Complete the following activities:

- *List at least 100 people you could ask for a lead.* Begin assembling your database now, so you can remember these and others you speak with. They are your future business goldmine. Besides adding these people to your database, attach an "alarm" on their names so you remember to call them, send them notes, and so on. Real estate-specific contract management programs include

FIGURE 4.1   Your Weekly Plan (Complete Each Week)

Name: _____

Week: _____

Time	Monday	Tuesday	Wednesday	Thursday	Friday	Saturday	Sunday
7–8							
8–9							
9–10							
10–11							
11–12							
12–1							
1–2							
2–3							
3–4							
4–5							
5–6							
6–7							
7–8							
8–9							

FIGURE 4.2   Joan's Weekly Plan—First Week

Week: _____ One   Name: _____ Joan Smith

Time	Monday	Tuesday	Wednesday	Thursday	Friday	Saturday	Sunday
7–8	Organize desk		Day off	Write 40 follow-up cards			
8–9	Office meeting	Paperwork			Meet w/mgr	Paperwork	
9–10	Office tour	Call 20 people I know		Call 10 people to ask for leads	Call 20 people to ask for leads	Show homes	Show homes
10–11	→	→		→	→	→	→
11–12		Floor time		Paperwork	Inspect		
12–1	Office orient.	Lunch		Lunch	Lunch	Lunch	Lunch
1–2	Inspect inventory	Start market analysis		Inspect inventory	Inspect	Floor time	Follow-up
2–3	→	→		→	Continue mkt. analysis	→	Visits
3–4	Call people I know	Follow-up		Follow-up	→	Inspect inventory	
4–5	List 100 people to ask for leads	Inspect inventory		Meet with loan officer	Circle prospect 25 homes	Circle prospect 25 homes	
5–6	→	→	- - - →	→	→	→	→
6–7							
7–8							Do listing presentation
8–9							→

FIGURE 4.3   Daily Planner

Date:_____

Priorities: Accomplished   Notes:

1._____   ☐   _____

2._____   ☐   _____

3._____   ☐   _____

4._____   ☐   _____

5._____   ☐   _____

6._____   ☐   _____

7._____   ☐   _____

8._____   ☐   _____

9._____   ☐   _____

10._____   ☐   _____

	Contacts	Qualified Leads	Listing Appointments	Showings
Activity				

	Listings Obtained	Sales	Listings Sold
Results			

FIGURE 4.3   Daily Planner

Date:_____

Priorities: Accomplished   Notes:

1._____   ☐   _____

2._____   ☐   _____

3._____   ☐   _____

4._____   ☐   _____

5._____   ☐   _____

6._____   ☐   _____

7._____   ☐   _____

8._____   ☐   _____

9._____   ☐   _____

10._____   ☐   _____

	Contacts	Qualified Leads	Listing Appointments	Showings
Activity				

	Listings Obtained	Sales	Listings Sold
Results			

FIGURE 4.3   Daily Planner

Date:_____

Priorities: Accomplished   Notes:

1._____   ☐   _____

2._____   ☐   _____

3._____   ☐   _____

4._____   ☐   _____

5._____   ☐   _____

6._____   ☐   _____

7._____   ☐   _____

8._____   ☐   _____

9._____   ☐   _____

10._____   ☐   _____

	Contacts	Qualified Leads	Listing Appointments	Showings
Activity				

	Listings Obtained	Sales	Listings Sold
Results			

FIGURE 4.3   Daily Planner

Date:_____

Priorities: Accomplished   Notes:

1._____   ☐   _____
2._____   ☐   _____
3._____   ☐   _____
4._____   ☐   _____
5._____   ☐   _____
6._____   ☐   _____
7._____   ☐   _____
8._____   ☐   _____
9._____   ☐   _____
10._____   ☐   _____

	Contacts	Qualified Leads	Listing Appointments	Showings
Activity				

	Listings Obtained	Sales	Listings Sold
Results			

ready-made "distribution plans" to help you decide how to follow up, along with pre-written letters and time frames—or you might wish to design your own. In any case, don't just make the call; plan the entire process with that contact—that's how sales income is ultimately made.

- *Using Sales Skill 1, craft a sales script to call on people you know.* See Sections 8 and 9 for information about this sales skill.
- *Using Sales Skill 3, ask for a lead.* See Sections 8 and 9 for information about this sales skill.
- *Call or see at least 50 people this week, and ask for a lead* using the three new sales skills.

Begin your *circle prospecting.* Choose an area to circle prospect in and a home to circle prospect around. (See Section 8 for more information on circle prospecting.) Complete the following activities:

- Craft a sales call for circle prospecting using three new sales skills.
- Circle prospect at least 50 homes. Ask for a lead.

Aim for the following results through your prospecting:

- Two secured, qualified buyer leads
- Two secured, qualified seller leads
- At least two showings to customers
- One scheduled listing presentation

Be sure to log qualified buyers and sellers into the grids in Section 10 on pages 146 and 148.

Before beginning your assignments for Section 4, log in your prospecting and results on the grids in Section 12 on page 154. Each day log in your actuals, and tally them at the end of the week. Carry your goals and actuals to Figure 4.4—*Week One: Accomplishments*—and log them in. Compare goals with actuals. See Figure 4.5—*Joan's First Week: 30 Days to Dollars*—for a prototype prospecting plan.

Business Support

Become comfortable with the office operation. Ask your manager or office manager for an orientation checklist. Read the office operations manual, if one is available. Become acquainted with all support materials.

FIGURE 4.4   Week One: Accomplishments

Business Development

Assignments	Completed	Manager's Comments
30 Days to Dollars Activities (Figure 12.3)	_____	_____
From Your Scorecard (Figure 12.4)	_____	_____

Buyers

Qualified Buyers:_____	_____	_____
Buyer Tours:_____	_____	_____
Sales:_____	_____	_____

Sellers

Qualified Listing Presentations:_____	_____	_____
Qualified Listings:_____	_____	_____
Listings Sold:_____	_____	_____

Buyer/seller qualifiers in Section 10 have been completed:_____

Business Support

Assignments	Completed	Manager's Comments
	_____	_____
	_____	_____
	_____	_____
Preparations for Reactive Activities	_____	_____
	_____	_____
	_____	_____
	_____	_____
	_____	_____

Take these numbers from your grids (see Figures 12.3 and 12.4). The numbers you create will form the basis for your analysis of your personal ratios of calls to leads to appointments to sales. By keeping these numbers, you are becoming an effective manager of your own business-development program.

FIGURE 4.5   Joan's First Week: 30 Days to Dollars

Activity	Weekly Minimum
1. Contact people you know/meet.	
In-person calls	20
Phone calls	30
Follow-up (phone calls, mail, e-mail, etc.)	50

Joan contacts 50 people.

2. Circle prospect in person.	25

Joan circle prospects 25 homes.

3. Choose one additional activity from these.	
Farm Area in-person contacts	50
or	
FSBOs in-person or phone contacts	25
or	
Expired listings in-person or phone contacts	25

4. Hold public open houses.	1

Joan holds 1 open house.

Total weekly Minimum in-person/phone contacts: 100-125

Learn the basics of financing and qualifying. Meet with a loan officer. Set as many appointments as you wish with the loan officer until you are comfortable with the basics.

Complete a market analysis on your own home. Package it. Practice your presentation of your market analysis. Inspect three agents' market analyses, and include their best points in your package. Create three visual methods to counter sellers' objections to pricing.

Preparation for Reactive Prospective Activities

Most offices provide scheduling for two reactive prospecting activities, in which agents wait for prospects to come to them:

1. Floor time
2. Public open houses

Plan for no more than 20 percent of your leads to come from reactive activities!

To prepare to begin these activities:

- *Observe two different people holding floor time in your office.* Inspect the resource materials available. Gather information on how agents handle calls and objections. Find any resources—articles, books, audiotapes—in your office that show you how to handle floor calls. Practice securing the appointment with a friend. Role-play various sales situations.
- *Observe two public open houses this weekend.* Make notes on the strategies you think are good; those that are bad. Interview three agents on how they prepare for and hold open houses. Learn five strategies they use to control the prospect to secure an appointment.

Final Thoughts for Week One

If you are like many new agents, at the end of Week One your brain feels like mush. New words, new systems, unfamiliar territory—no wonder that new agents may re-evaluate their charge-ahead attitude and decide to ease into the career! They reason that they must spend more time on learning, on research, on organization—instead of talking to people so quickly. Their confidence decreases as rejection increases. New agents conclude that to increase their confidence they need more knowledge.

Build Real, Lasting Confidence

Up and Running is designed to build your confidence the right way—through increasing your skills. Real estate is a performance art, not a knowledge pursuit; true confidence in real estate is built from successful performance. However, until you perform, you have only your practice and imagination to build your confidence. Although there are methods to increase your confidence mentally, they pale before the reality of a great performance.

Practice

It's painful to learn from your mistakes with real customers. However, there's another effective way to learn skills—practice. All too often, the value of practice is underestimated by both agents and managers. But it's worth the effort to role-play each segment that requires sales communication with people:

- Prospecting scenarios
- Counseling/qualifying buyer scenarios
- Showing and closing buyer scenarios
- Presenting and negotiating offer scenarios
- Qualifying seller scenarios
- Marketing/presentation scenarios
- Price reduction/review scenarios

Agents believe that because they can talk they can sell. But we have already discussed the realities of conversation versus the special communication skills required for sales success. I guarantee that if you take seriously the practice asked of you in *Up and Running,* your performance with people will improve quickly and your confidence will soar. Every successful salesperson I have known who started quickly in this business organized, systematized, practiced, and perfected each step in the sales cycle.

Perfect Practice Makes Perfect

The best kind of practice increases your skill and results. Back to my piano-practicing days: As a four-year-old, I picked out tunes on the keys and added the chords. I could play pop music reasonably well. Then, at age six, I started piano lessons. As I progressed to more demanding piano teachers, I learned that "faking it 'til you made it" just would not meet their standards. In fact, my best piano teacher,

Mr. Green, taught me to practice very slowly, *so there weren't any mistakes.* I found that if I practiced quickly, I practiced my mistakes right along with the rest of the piece.

Although practice was tedious, by using Mr. Green's method I became a much better pianist. Too often, real estate agents practice the mistakes and end up with a sales system that is "more mistake than effective."

Thus, to optimize your practice, practice perfectly. Perfect practice makes perfect.

A Desire to Do It Again

If you have ever experienced the exhilaration of a fine performance, you know you want to run right out and do it again! Success is a great motivator. As we progress through Sections 4-7 we will be discussing self-motivation. For now, suffice it to say that good performance is the best motivator—and, correspondingly, the best motivator for selling is selling. This is the greatest reason to get out into the real estate field, even before you are comfortable: to motivate yourself to continue your quest for a successful real estate career.

5

Week Two

In Section 5 you will continue the business-producing activities introduced in Section 4—Week One—and you will incorporate one additional type of prospecting. Even though you may choose not to use some of the prospecting methods introduced here long term, you are expanding your skills. You are developing a prospecting repertoire. When I was in college, I worked my way through school playing piano in bars. I found that the more tunes and styles I could play, the more tips I made. Hence, I developed a wide repertoire. I never knew when it would come in handy. Having several prospecting skills available to you is your insurance plan against changing markets.

Besides learning some new sales skills in Week Two, you will start assembling your systems for controlling buyers and sellers.

Objectives

Business Development

- Continue *30 Days to Dollars* prospecting, adding one additional type of prospecting.
- Make 100 sales calls using the categories in *30 Days to Dollars*.
- Secure two qualified showing appointments.
- Secure one qualified listing appointment.
- Apply two new sales skills.

Business Support

- Assemble listing presentation materials.
- Assemble counseling packet for buyers, and buyer strategies.
- Write two purchase and sale agreements for practice.
- Continue your contact management system for prospects.
- Become proficient at prospecting skills in the categories added.
- Practice two new sales skills.

Weekly Activity Plan

Create your weekly plan, following the guidelines in Week One. Using Figure 5.1, log in your activities in the same order. Then, prioritize your weekly plan. Using Figure 5.2, log your prioritized activities into each of your daily plans. Following this same format for one month will create a success-building habit. You will never be the kind of agent who sits around the office waiting for someone to plan for you. As you accomplish your goals, log them into Figure 5.3, Week Two: Accomplishments.

Business Development

Continue the *30 Days to Dollars* plan discussed in Section 2 with the following activities:

- Call on at least 25 people you know. Ask for leads.
- Circle prospect at least 50 homes. Ask for leads.
- Call on 25 for-sale-by-owners or expired listings.

Refer to Sections 8 and 9 for additional information on these prospecting methods.

FIGURE 5.1   Your Weekly Plan

Week: _____

Name: _____

Time	Monday	Tuesday	Wednesday	Thursday	Friday	Saturday	Sunday
7–8							
8–9							
9–10							
10–11							
11–12							
12–1							
1–2							
2–3							
3–4							
4–5							
5–6							
6–7							
7–8							
8–9							

FIGURE 5.2   Daily Planner

Date:_____

Priorities: Accomplished   Notes:

1._____   ☐   _____
2._____   ☐   _____
3._____   ☐   _____
4._____   ☐   _____
5._____   ☐   _____
6._____   ☐   _____
7._____   ☐   _____
8._____   ☐   _____
9._____   ☐   _____
10._____   ☐   _____

	Contacts	Qualified Leads	Listing Appointments	Showings
Activity				

	Listings Obtained	Sales	Listings Sold
Results			

FIGURE 5.2 Daily Planner

Date:_____

Priorities: Accomplished   Notes:

1._____   ☐   _____

2._____   ☐   _____

3._____   ☐   _____

4._____   ☐   _____

5._____   ☐   _____

6._____   ☐   _____

7._____   ☐   _____

8._____   ☐   _____

9._____   ☐   _____

10._____   ☐   _____

	Contacts	Qualified Leads	Listing Appointments	Showings
Activity				

	Listings Obtained	Sales	Listings Sold
Results			

FIGURE 5.2   Daily Planner

Date:_____

Priorities: Accomplished   Notes:

1._____   ☐   _____

2._____   ☐   _____

3._____   ☐   _____

4._____   ☐   _____

5._____   ☐   _____

6._____   ☐   _____

7._____   ☐   _____

8._____   ☐   _____

9._____   ☐   _____

10._____   ☐   _____

	Contacts	Qualified Leads	Listing Appointments	Showings
Activity				

	Listings Obtained	Sales	Listings Sold
Results			

FIGURE 5.2   Daily Planner

Date:_____

Priorities: Accomplished   Notes:

1._____   ☐   _____

2._____   ☐   _____

3._____   ☐   _____

4._____   ☐   _____

5._____   ☐   _____

6._____   ☐   _____

7._____   ☐   _____

8._____   ☐   _____

9._____   ☐   _____

10._____   ☐   _____

	Contacts	Qualified Leads	Listing Appointments	Showings
Activity				

	Listings Obtained	Sales	Listings Sold
Results			

FIGURE 5.2   Daily Planner

Date:_____

Priorities: Accomplished   Notes:

1._____   ☐   _____

2._____   ☐   _____

3._____   ☐   _____

4._____   ☐   _____

5._____   ☐   _____

6._____   ☐   _____

7._____   ☐   _____

8._____   ☐   _____

9._____   ☐   _____

10._____   ☐   _____

	Contacts	Qualified Leads	Listing Appointments	Showings
Activity				

	Listings Obtained	Sales	Listings Sold
Results			

FIGURE 5.2   Daily Planner

Date:_____

Priorities: Accomplished   Notes:

1._____   ☐   _____
2._____   ☐   _____
3._____   ☐   _____
4._____   ☐   _____
5._____   ☐   _____
6._____   ☐   _____
7._____   ☐   _____
8._____   ☐   _____
9._____   ☐   _____
10._____   ☐   _____

	Contacts	Qualified Leads	Listing Appointments	Showings
Activity				

	Listings Obtained	Sales	Listings Sold
Results			

FIGURE 5.3   Week Two: Accomplishments

Business Development

Assignments	Completed	Manager's Comments
30 Days to Dollars Activities (Figure 12.3)	_____	_____
From Your Scorecard (Figure 12.4)	_____	_____

Buyers

Qualified Buyers:_____	_____	_____
Buyer Tours:_____	_____	_____
Sales:_____	_____	_____

Sellers

Qualified Listing Presentations:_____	_____	_____
Qualified Listings:_____	_____	_____
Listings Sold:_____	_____	_____

Buyer/seller qualifiers in Section 10 have been completed:_____

Business Support

Assignments	Completed	Manager's Comments
	_____	_____
	_____	_____
	_____	_____
	_____	_____
	_____	_____
	_____	_____
	_____	_____

Take these numbers from your grids (see Figures 12.3 and 12.4). The numbers you create will form the basis for your analysis of your personal ratios of calls to leads to appointments to sales. By keeping these numbers, you are becoming an effective manager of your own business-development program.

Hold one public open house this weekend. To prepare and develop the best strategies, talk to three people in your office. (This is a reactive strategy. However, you will secure leads by calling on the homeowners around this home prior to the open house, or by circle prospecting.)

Refer to Figure 5.4, *Joan's Second Week: 30 Days to Dollars,* the prototype prospecting plan you should be following now.

Continue using Sales Skills 1, 2, and 3 (see Sections 8 and 9) as you prospect and work with buyers and sellers. Add Sales Skill 4: Objection Busters—Using the AAA Method. (Refer to Sections 8 and 9 in this book for more information.) Craft an *objection-buster* to the three common objections you get when you are prospecting. Practice answering these objections using the AAA method (see Sections 8 and 9). Use this method to counter your three most common objections as you prospect this week.

Before beginning your Week Two business-developing activities, log in your goals (see Figures 12.3 and 12.4).

From prospecting, you should strive to obtain the following results:

- Two qualified buyer appointments
- Two showing appointments with buyers
- Two qualified seller leads
- One qualified listing presentation

If you do not get these results from your prospecting, increase the number of calls you make.

Log your qualified buyers and sellers into your grids (see Figures 10.1, 10.2, 10.3 and 10.4) Be sure these people are qualified, so that you are not wasting your time.

Business Support

Clarify the portions and systems in your listing process. Review the pattern of the listing process (from your initial training program or from interviewing agents in your office). Gather the materials for the entire listing process. Decide which materials to use for your first visit, the marketing part of your presentation, and your pricing presentation.

Review three agents' presentations. Take notes on the strategies you want to incorporate, and assemble your listing process materials.

For more information on the complete listing process, see the References section of this book. Especially relevant for you is *The Client-Based Marketing System,* for it shows you exactly how to assemble a complete listing process. Also, *On Track to Success in 30 Days* has

FIGURE 5.4 Joan's Second Week: 30 Days to Dollars

Activity	Weekly Minimum
1. Contact people you know/meet.	
In-person calls	20
Phone calls	30
Follow-up (phone calls, mail, e-mail, etc.)	50
Joan contacts 50 people.	
2. Circle prospect in person.	25
Joan circle prospects 25 homes.	
3. Choose one additional activity from these.	
Farm Area in-person contacts	50
or	
FSBOs in-person or phone contacts	25
or	
Expired listings in-person or phone contacts	25
Joan calls on 25 expired listings.	
4. Hold public open houses.	1
Joan holds 1 open house.	

Total weekly minimum in-person/phone contacts: **100-125**

dozens of checklists and analytical tools for agents' use in refining their systems.

Using Sales Skill 4: The AAA method to craft objection-busters, practice answering three common seller objections to listing with you. Create three visuals to substantiate your information.

Clarify and assemble the portions and systems of the buying process. Interview three agents on the process and materials they use to counsel and qualify a buyer prior to putting the buyer in the car. (Include a strategy and materials on asking for a buyer's loyalty, as well as a discussion and materials concerning Agency disclosure.) Assemble these materials into a buyer's packet—a professional resource for helping a buyer through the buying process. For more information on creating buyers' presentations, see the Reference section in this book. *The Complete Buyers' Agent Tool Ki*t shows agents exactly how to create presentations and processes for buyers that provide added value and loyalty.

Using Sales Skill 4, interview the agents on the three most common objections buyers have to buying, and how these agents handle those objections. Using the AAA method to crafting objection-busters, craft your strategy for handling these objections. Create three visuals you will need to substantiate your claims.

Write two purchase and sale agreements. Practice writing purchase and sale agreements, so that you will be comfortable writing the actual agreements. Include a practice agreement for purchasing the property you currently own, and one using a method to purchase other than conventional financing.

Create your contact management system. Investigate and organize your contact management system. Interview three agents to learn how they organize their prospects, customers, and clients. Decide on a system—manual or computer—and start it this week.

Continue logging your contacts into your contact management system. Add fields as needed. See three agents and interview them to see how they organize their prospects, customers and clients.

Decide on your follow-up plan and use it with each prospect you meet.

Final Thoughts for Week Two

If you have been prospecting consistently, you have probably found some buyers to qualify. Hopefully, you have even shown houses to a few buyers this week. On the listing side, you have no doubt found at least one homeowner who was interested in selling his or her home. You have made one listing presentation. As the list grows and opportunities increase, you begin to experience some *time management* challenges. To help you manage your time, try the solutions recommended in the following paragraphs.

Continue Your Weekly Plan

It's amazing how many agents don't plan their week—ahead of their week! In fact, from teaching sales skill workshops, I have found that less than ten percent of experienced agents actually lay out a week's work in advance. When they look at what they have accomplished the prior month, they are stunned. From analyzing their prior month's activities, they discover that they have been nonproductive because they:

- let non-income-producing activities dominate their schedule;
- allowed well-meaning people to steal their time; and
- placed too much emphasis on support activities.

They became their own assistants! However, with new insights, agents can get back on track and create a plan that helps them reach their goals. *Up and Running* teaches you, from the beginning, how to prioritize your activities so that you can avoid this common mistake.

Don't Stop Prospecting

There is one sure way to create a low-producing career: Stop prospecting when you are busy with other activities. As my friend Bill Feldman says, "When you stop pedaling the bicycle, you fall off." Pedaling the bicycle fast enough to stay on track simply means planning, executing. and monitoring your business-developing plan (prospecting) to provide you with enough new leads to give you the results that will meet your goals.

Following the Leader—Who's the Leader?   How much money do you think, on average, a REALTOR® makes? According to surveys, the public thinks agents make about $60,000. Actually, it's about half that—less than $30,000, which in most areas translates to about 13 transactions a year. (That's for all REALTORS®, regardless of the number of years they have been in the business.) Is that more or less than you expect of yourself in your first year? The point is this: If you expect to complete more than 12 transactions your first year, do not follow the example of most real estate agents.

Who have you modeled your weekly plan after? Be sure it's a producer who has attained your expectations. If not, you will find yourself unwittingly performing many support activities, drinking coffee, gossiping, and *not* creating a successful real estate career.

Ask Yourself: What Do I Need to Do to Get into Action?

Accumulating knowledge as a confidence builder is a common mistake new agents make. Ned (not his real name) was an example of this. In the business eight months, Ned had earned $2,000. He was in the office regularly and appeared busy with paperwork. He attended law courses and was well-informed on financing. One day I saw Ned collating maps. I asked him what he was doing. He explained that he was putting together a series of maps for a buyer's tour. I thought that was exceptional; buyers would really want to know the whereabouts of the homes they were seeing. Unfortunately, Ned had used his strategy with only two buyers—that's all the buyers he had put in his car in the past three months! He had spent his time on this nifty map system, but had not talked to enough people to get them into the car—or have the opportunity to appreciate the map system! Which is more important to your goal attainment—talking to people, qualifying them and showing them homes, or working diligently on a map system (so you will be prepared) in case you find someone who wants you to show them homes?

How Do You "Get into Action"? In a wonderful book, *The Conative Connection,* Kathy Kolbe explores the ways different personalities get into action—not how we learn, but how we get into action. Some people barge ahead and worry about the details later. We start badly, but, because we're tenacious, we surprise people by how good we finally get. Unfortunately, our supervisors often remember only how bad we were when we started. We must be tough-minded and keep at it; we must retain an image of ourselves as "finished products," because others will not see us that way. Other people observe the action for a long time. Finally, when we feel ready to perform well, we get into action. We start slowly but well. Because of our slow start, we don't get much positive reinforcement from our supervisors (or coach or manager), who notes our lack of progress compared with others in the office. If slow starters are tenacious and believe in themselves, they become very good because they practice perfectly. Kolbe points out several "get into action" styles. This book will help you pinpoint your "get into action" style as well as the barriers and challenges you face as you start your real estate career.

Go Ahead—Be Embarrassed. There is no way to be experienced until you get experience. No agents like to take risks, to be embarrassed, to have buyers and sellers guess that they are new in the business. But face it—everyone has been new in the business. Just go ahead and get those first few months over with. You will be embarrassed every day—many times. As a new agent, my most common statement to buyers or sellers was: "I don't know, but I'll find out." In music little could stump me—but in real estate *anything* could stump me! Still, I muddled through it, and you will, too.

Taking Your Time. I wish I could tell you that you can successfully launch your real estate career by taking lots of time to "get ready." However, if you take all the time in the world, you will fail for three reasons:

1. *Real estate is a performance art.* It doesn't matter how much you know; it only matters how you interact with people. And that takes practice. To remember and emulate good performance, we need to perform right after we have heard, seen, and practiced that performance. Learning something in a class and letting that skill lie dormant for months just guarantees poor skill—and high stress.

2. *The only true motivator is selling.* Tell me that you're in no hurry, that you have plenty of time to make your first sale. I predict, that, within three months, you'll be mentally, if not physically, out of real estate. It's tough to stay motivated without some positive reinforcement. The longer it takes you to make a sale, the more reasons you will find to leave the business.

3. *Your mentors, your manager, and perhaps your adviser will lose interest in you.* Because they don't see you taking meaningful action steps, your mentors will naturally become less motivated to help you. For you to stay motivated, you need the positive support of your mentors. From my experience, it takes about two months for managers and mentors to lose interest in a new agent. If I don't see a lot of prospecting and working with people within that first two months, I turn my attention to other agents who are creating activities. It's difficult and time-consuming to constantly think of new ways to motivate agents after they are deflated—again!

Straight Ahead and Strive for Tone

As this old musical saying aptly describes, at the beginning of your career, doing it is more important than preparing to do it—or knowing about it. Do it the best you can—and you'll learn how to do it better. Now, on to your third week in the business!

6

Week Three

This week you will again add to your prospecting and sales skill repertoire. To gain confidence in purchase and sale agreements, you will write some agreements using different methods of financing. To increase your credibility with buyers and sellers, make these exercises challenging.

Even though you are new in the business, now is the time to set yourself apart from the crowd. You will begin to do so in this week's assignments.

Objectives

Business Development

- Complete 100 sales calls, including using one new contact method.
- Secure two qualified buyer leads.
- Secure two qualified seller leads.
- Show homes to two qualified buyer groups.
- Attend two listing appointments.
- List one marketable property.
- Apply one new sales skill.

Business Support

- Learn two methods of writing purchase and sale agreements, using alternative methods of financing, including one offer contingent on the sale of the purchaser's home.
- Create personal promotion pieces, including a professional portfolio (agent promotional brochure, or "friendly" resume). See the References section for information on assembling a portfolio.
- Create a follow-up plan that ties into a contact management plan for recontacting leads to date.
- Gain performance excellence with Sales Skill 5.
- Create performance excellence in handling objections through crafting three more objection-busters with visuals.
- Continue your contact management follow-up plan to ensure long-term relationships and referrals.

Weekly Activity Plan

Create your weekly plan, following the guidelines in Week One. Using Figure 6.1, prioritize your activities. Log them into your daily planners (see Figure 6.2). Set your goals, and keep track of your "actuals" in Section 12. Record your accomplishments for this week in Figure 6.3.

FIGURE 6.1   Your Weekly Plan

Week: _____

Name: _____

Time	Monday	Tuesday	Wednesday	Thursday	Friday	Saturday	Sunday
7–8							
8–9							
9–10							
10–11							
11–12							
12–1							
1–2							
2–3							
3–4							
4–5							
5–6							
6–7							
7–8							
8–9							

FIGURE 6.2   Daily Planner

Date:_____

Priorities: Accomplished   Notes:

1._____   ☐   _____

2._____   ☐   _____

3._____   ☐   _____

4._____   ☐   _____

5._____   ☐   _____

6._____   ☐   _____

7._____   ☐   _____

8._____   ☐   _____

9._____   ☐   _____

10._____   ☐   _____

	Contacts	Qualified Leads	Listing Appointments	Showings
Activity				

	Listings Obtained	Sales	Listings Sold
Results			

FIGURE 6.2   Daily Planner

Date:_____

Priorities: Accomplished   Notes:

1._____   ☐   _____
2._____   ☐   _____
3._____   ☐   _____
4._____   ☐   _____
5._____   ☐   _____
6._____   ☐   _____
7._____   ☐   _____
8._____   ☐   _____
9._____   ☐   _____
10._____   ☐   _____

	Contacts	Qualified Leads	Listing Appointments	Showings
Activity				

	Listings Obtained	Sales	Listings Sold
Results			

FIGURE 6.2   Daily Planner

Date:_____

Priorities: Accomplished   Notes:

1._____   ☐   _____

2._____   ☐   _____

3._____   ☐   _____

4._____   ☐   _____

5._____   ☐   _____

6._____   ☐   _____

7._____   ☐   _____

8._____   ☐   _____

9._____   ☐   _____

10._____   ☐   _____

	Contacts	Qualified Leads	Listing Appointments	Showings
Activity				

	Listings Obtained	Sales	Listings Sold
Results			

FIGURE 6.2   Daily Planner

Date:_____

Priorities:	Accomplished	Notes:

1._____ ☐   _____
2._____ ☐   _____
3._____ ☐   _____
4._____ ☐   _____
5._____ ☐   _____
6._____ ☐   _____
7._____ ☐   _____
8._____ ☐   _____
9._____ ☐   _____
10._____ ☐   _____

	Contacts	Qualified Leads	Listing Appointments	Showings
Activity				

	Listings Obtained	Sales	Listings Sold
Results			

FIGURE 6.2   Daily Planner

Date:_____

Priorities: Accomplished   Notes:

1._____   ☐   _____
2._____   ☐   _____
3._____   ☐   _____
4._____   ☐   _____
5._____   ☐   _____
6._____   ☐   _____
7._____   ☐   _____
8._____   ☐   _____
9._____   ☐   _____
10._____   ☐   _____

	Contacts	Qualified Leads	Listing Appointments	Showings
Activity				

	Listings Obtained	Sales	Listings Sold
Results			

FIGURE 6.2   Daily Planner

Date:_____

Priorities: Accomplished   Notes:

1._____   ☐   _____

2._____   ☐   _____

3._____   ☐   _____

4._____   ☐   _____

5._____   ☐   _____

6._____   ☐   _____

7._____   ☐   _____

8._____   ☐   _____

9._____   ☐   _____

10._____   ☐   _____

	Contacts	Qualified Leads	Listing Appointments	Showings
Activity				

	Listings Obtained	Sales	Listings Sold
Results			

FIGURE 6.3   Week Three: Accomplishments

Business Development

Assignments	Completed	Manager's Comments
***30 Days to Dollars* Activities** (Figure 12.3)	_____	_____
From Your Scorecard (Figure 12.4)	_____	_____

Buyers

Qualified Buyers: _____	_____	_____
Buyer Tours: _____	_____	_____
Sales: _____	_____	_____

Sellers

Qualified Listing Presentations:_____	_____	_____
Qualified Listings:_____	_____	_____
Listings Sold:_____	_____	_____

Buyer/seller qualifiers in Section 10 have been completed:_____

Business Support

Assignments	Completed	Manager's Comments
	_____	_____
	_____	_____
	_____	_____
	_____	_____
	_____	_____
	_____	_____
	_____	_____

Take these numbers from your grids (see Figures 12.3 and 12.4) so that you can start your own self-management program. The numbers you create will form the basis for your analysis of your personal ratios of calls to leads to appointments to sales. By keeping these numbers, you are becoming an effective manager of your own business-development program.

FIGURE 6.4   Joan's Third Week: 30 Days to Dollars

Activity	Weekly Minimum
1. Contact people you know/meet.	
In-person calls	20
Phone calls	30
Follow-up (phone calls, mail, e-mail, etc.)	50

Joan contacts 50 people.

2. Circle prospect in person.	25

Joan circle prospects 25 homes.

3. Choose one additional activity from these.		
Farm Area	in-person contacts	50
	or	
FSBOs	in-person or phone contacts	25
	or	
Expired listings	in-person or phone contacts	25

4. Hold public open houses.	1

Joan holds 1 open house.

Total weekly minimum in-person/phone contacts: 100-125

Business Development

Make 100 sales calls, using the *30 Days to Dollars* priorities of target markets and numbers. Choose the markets you will call on. Make the second call to the for-sale-by-owners or expired listings that you began last week.

See Figure 6.4—*Joan Smith's Third Week: 30 Days to Dollars*—for a prototype prospecting plan. Your plan should look similar.

Strive to achieve the following business-development results:

• Secure two qualified buyer appointments.

• Show homes to two qualified buyer groups.

• Secure two appointments to do a listing presentation.

• List one marketable property.

If your numbers of prospects are not providing the leads you need, increase your numbers of prospects. Log in your qualified buyers and sellers using the grids in Section 10.

Apply Sales Skill 5, the "hum technique." Refer to Sections 8 and 9 for more information. Use this technique in your prospecting and qualifying conversations with buyers and sellers.

Business Support

Create reasons for people to choose you. Substantiate them in writing. Prepare a professional portfolio or brochure to promote yourself. Ask three agents in your office for ideas on promotional pieces and/or the portfolio. For more information on assembling a portfolio, see the reference section of this book (*Your Professional Portfolio*).

Increase your skill with purchase and sale agreements. Write two purchase and sale agreements using alternative financing methods. Make one offer contingent on the sale of a purchaser's home. Check these offers with your manager to be sure that you are using all the wordings and addenda available to you.

Practice the systemization trend by continuing your business follow-through. Continue your follow-up program. Work your follow-up plan for re-communicating with your leads regularly. Your plan should now include when leads are contacted, how these leads are contacted, the script used, the materials included, and the objective of the call. Put the dates to contact in your daily planner or in your contact management program.

Final Thoughts for Week Three

By now, you should be developing the success habits that new agents need to ensure a fast-starting career. The exciting part—and the part you will not appreciate for another year—is that you have subconsciously created a job description that is different from that of most agents. Your job description is centered around the business of real estate—not the research of real estate. Unfortunately, many agents start their real estate careers in a research mode—trying to find out all there is to know about the field. These agents become known for their knowledge. People compliment them on their understanding of finance and their accumulation of property information; people use this information. Because it is human nature for people to continue what they get rewarded or complimented for, these agents continue accumulating knowledge!

Be Certain about What You Want

You are learning good habits that lead to creating a productive business. You are correctly prioritizing your activities in order to build the right job description. Continue these success habits, and you will become known as a salesperson.

It's easy to slip into a different job description and become known for something other than production. John (not his real name) was an agent in the first office I managed. When I was still working as an agent, I admired John's depth of information about waterfront property and asked him to share his information with me. John was happy to help me out. I realized that John wasn't very successful, yet I considered that his business. Later, when I became manager of the office, I discovered that John was completing only six transactions a year— in his third year in the business—not enough to continue to build his business or support our office image as full-time, committed professionals. Yet John, who had received positive reinforcement for his *knowledge,* was content. As we had established standards of excellence in our office (which included production minimums), it was my job as a manager to work with John to help him increase his production. Working together, John and I agreed that, for him to stay with our office, he would have to change his job description. This, admittedly, would be difficult, because he had been encouraged to sustain his reputation as *a waterfront expert.* In fact, it proved impossible—John liked the comfort of collating more than the excitement of selling real estate.

Create the Future—Your Way

You have been in the business three weeks. Is your image of yourself different from the one you had when you started in this business? Successful performers have learned to create a "completed" picture of themselves as great performers—*long before they* are *terrific performers.* This helps them to predict the outcome of their efforts. If you don't know where you're going, you can't get there!

Lou Tice, the founder of Pacific Institute, calls this skill *self-efficacy.* It is the ability to create yourself as a finished "product" in your head and hold that image, even though no one in the outside world has a clue that you are going to end up that way. What a skill! This technique is practiced in karate. When our son, Chris, took karate lessons he first, he watched great performers—black belts—performing the *katas* (fighting moves in a format) and *kumite* (actual fighting). Then he envisioned himself performing each part of these moves, then connected the complete picture. Finally, he performed the moves, very slowly, *practicing perfectly.* He was coached every step of the way to ensure that he was practicing perfectly. After he perfected each move in context, he practiced performing faster. This method of creating perfect performance resulted in his winning medals in national and international competition—even while experiencing great growth spurts. His developed skill of self-efficacy ensured that his mind would hold the picture of his perfect performance. This skill has proved to be invaluable throughout his life.

Develop the Professional "You"

Take a few minutes in a quiet place by yourself. Imagine yourself as the successful real estate agent you intend to be. What will you do? What kind of recognition and power will you gain? What affiliations will you make that reflect your ideal of yourself as a pro? Create a movie with you as the star, complete with the movement, color, dialogue, tastes, and smells. Make it fun, exciting, and rewarding—in color. Play it over and over in your head—20 times a day for a month. Doing this will counteract your "growth spurts"—objections, barriers, negative self-talk, lost leads—as you start your career. You must develop some *mental ammunition.* Remember, people treat you as they see you. They can't see the new movie you have created until you start acting it out. Even then, they will try to put you back into your "old movie." It's human nature. Unwittingly, we help our friends fail by not becoming supporting players in their new picture. You must have a strong movie to move yourself in the direction you want to go, so that others can get caught up in the new action and let go of the old.

Show That You're the Professional of Choice

Recently, an agent who had been in the business about a year told me she couldn't get people who came to her open houses to appreciate her belief that she could help them. The reason she couldn't get them to appreciate her was that she didn't have time to engage them in conversation—to show them that she was knowledgeable and caring. Before she could talk to them, they were inching out the door. Her problem, stated in context of self-efficacy, was that she wasn't able to play her "movie as a pro" for people. But how could she? The public comes into open houses with three objectives:

1. To see the home
2. To get information
3. To avoid the salesperson

What does the public think about real estate salespeople? Generally, that one is as good as another. In training courses, I ask agents how they are different from the public's general view of a real estate agent. The reply is usually: "I'm an honest, enthusiastic, service-oriented professional." Then I ask the students how they *demonstrate* these qualities. The reply: "I demonstrate my qualities through the way I act with buyers and sellers." Here's the problem—people attending an open house want to avoid you, not get to know you. They will not give you the time to see you in the actions that prove your qualities. Unless you can *quickly* show them you are a cut above the "generic" agent, they will attempt an escape, just as they have with the other ten agents whose homes they have visited.

Project the Professional "You"

How do professionals in other fields demonstrate their professional selves? Envision your doctor's office. On the walls are diplomas that give you confidence about the doctor's qualifications. How do restaurants demonstrate—*before you eat the food*—that their food and service is good? Reviews from the newspaper, testimonials from customers. You can inspire confidence in your services by adopting some of the same promotional strategies that successful professionals and businesses use. In this week's assignments, you were to start developing your professional portfolio. For detailed information about exactly how to develop and use this portfolio, refer to *Your Professional Portfolio* listed in the Reference section. You will learn how to create a strong portfolio that will compete with that of any experienced agent.

Screen Your Movie—Increase Your Confidence

Developing a portfolio provides an additional benefit. During the development process, you complete exercises that help you develop your unique approach to the business. You draw on your particular strengths, services, and business approaches that differentiate you from the "generic" agent. You then project these in a pictorial way to communicate added value to the potential client or customer. The result is an overall promotional strategy that will compete successfully in the marketplace. The best news, for you, the new agent, is that this process helps develop your "movie" and greatly increases your confidence level.

Remember: It's not the finished portfolio, but the process of thinking through your strengths, challenges and competitors that is most important. In the highly competitive world of real estate sales and management, you must have a clearly, precisely defined picture of you as a "cut above." To compete you must create, define, refine, and promote yourself masterfully. The bonus to you is that you will have created your "movie!" (For more about this movie concept, see *The Real Estate Agent's Business Planning Guide.*) Then, when you are facing those barriers and losing the vividness of your movie, simply open your portfolio and remind yourself of the special qualities, strengths, and behaviors that propelled you into this business.

7

Week Four

You are now approaching your final week in the *Up and Running* activity plan. This week you will continue making the sales calls to create early success. You will refine your sellers' and buyers' presentations. You will add to your portfolio. These systems should be on their way to being professional, polished and practiced by now to ensure your success at every point of contact. (Note: As a pro, you will always be refining and tinkering with your systems. The objective in the first month is to get them to the point where you can use them as presentation guides.)

Objectives

Business Development

- Make 100 sales calls, using the methods that have proved to be most successful for you.
- Secure two qualified listing appointments.
- Secure two qualified showing appointments.
- Sell one home.
- Apply two new sales skills.

Business Support

- Complete the entire listing-process materials, including a market analysis package. Include eight visuals to counter common listing objections.
- Review and complete your counseling packet for buyers, including visuals for countering buyers' eight most common objections.
- Complete your personal promotional materials—a professional portfolio and/or your personal brochure.
- Gain performance excellence in two new sales skills.
- Continue your contact management data entry.

Weekly Activity Plan

Create your weekly plan, using the guidelines in Week One activity assignment (see Figure 7.1). Log in your activities and successes using Figures 7.2 and 7.3.

Business Development

Using the *30 Days to Dollars* plan, make 100 sales calls, using the methods that have proven most successful for you. Review the information in Sections 8 and 9 to sharpen your skills. Make the third call

FIGURE 7.1   Your Weekly Plan

Name: _____

Week: _____

Time	Monday	Tuesday	Wednesday	Thursday	Friday	Saturday	Sunday
7–8							
8–9							
9–10							
10–11							
11–12							
12–1							
1–2							
2–3							
3–4							
4–5							
5–6							
6–7							
7–8							
8–9							

FIGURE 7.2   Daily Planner

Date:_____

Priorities: Accomplished   Notes:

1._____   ☐   _____
2._____   ☐   _____
3._____   ☐   _____
4._____   ☐   _____
5._____   ☐   _____
6._____   ☐   _____
7._____   ☐   _____
8._____   ☐   _____
9._____   ☐   _____
10._____   ☐   _____

	Contacts	Qualified Leads	Listing Appointments	Showings
Activity				

	Listings Obtained	Sales	Listings Sold
Results			

FIGURE 7.2   Daily Planner

Date:_____

Priorities: Accomplished   Notes:

1._____   ☐   _____
2._____   ☐   _____
3._____   ☐   _____
4._____   ☐   _____
5._____   ☐   _____
6._____   ☐   _____
7._____   ☐   _____
8._____   ☐   _____
9._____   ☐   _____
10._____   ☐   _____

Activity	Contacts	Qualified Leads	Listing Appointments	Showings

Results	Listings Obtained	Sales	Listings Sold

FIGURE 7.2   Daily Planner

Date:_____

Priorities: Accomplished   Notes:

1._____   ☐   _____
2._____   ☐   _____
3._____   ☐   _____
4._____   ☐   _____
5._____   ☐   _____
6._____   ☐   _____
7._____   ☐   _____
8._____   ☐   _____
9._____   ☐   _____
10._____   ☐   _____

	Contacts	Qualified Leads	Listing Appointments	Showings
Activity				

	Listings Obtained	Sales	Listings Sold
Results			

FIGURE 7.2   Daily Planner

Date:_____

Priorities: Accomplished   Notes:

1._____   ☐   _____

2._____   ☐   _____

3._____   ☐   _____

4._____   ☐   _____

5._____   ☐   _____

6._____   ☐   _____

7._____   ☐   _____

8._____   ☐   _____

9._____   ☐   _____

10._____   ☐   _____

	Contacts	Qualified Leads	Listing Appointments	Showings
Activity				

	Listings Obtained	Sales	Listings Sold
Results			

FIGURE 7.2   Daily Planner

Date:_____

Priorities: Accomplished   Notes:

1._____   ☐   _____

2._____   ☐   _____

3._____   ☐   _____

4._____   ☐   _____

5._____   ☐   _____

6._____   ☐   _____

7._____   ☐   _____

8._____   ☐   _____

9._____   ☐   _____

10._____   ☐   _____

	Contacts	Qualified Leads	Listing Appointments	Showings
Activity				

	Listings Obtained	Sales	Listings Sold
Results			

FIGURE 7.2   Daily Planner

Date:_____

Priorities: Accomplished   Notes:

1._____   ☐   _____
2._____   ☐   _____
3._____   ☐   _____
4._____   ☐   _____
5._____   ☐   _____
6._____   ☐   _____
7._____   ☐   _____
8._____   ☐   _____
9._____   ☐   _____
10._____   ☐   _____

	Contacts	Qualified Leads	Listing Appointments	Showings
Activity				

	Listings Obtained	Sales	Listings Sold
Results			

FIGURE 7.3   Week Four: Accomplishments

Business Development

Assignments	Completed	Manager's Comments
30 Days to Dollars Activities (Figure 12.3)	_____	_____
From Your Scorecard (Figure 12.4)	_____	_____

Buyers

Qualified Buyers: _____	_____	_____
Buyer Tours:_____	_____	_____
Sales:_____	_____	_____

Sellers

Qualified Listing Presentations:_____	_____	_____
Qualified Listings:_____	_____	_____
Listings Sold:_____	_____	_____

Buyer/seller qualifiers in Section 10 have been completed:_____

Business Support

Assignments	Completed	Manager's Comments
	_____	_____
	_____	_____
Preparations for Reactive Activities	_____	_____
	_____	_____
	_____	_____
	_____	_____

Take these numbers from your grids (see Figures 12.3 and 12.4). The numbers you create will form the basis for your analysis of your personal ratios of calls to leads to appointments to sales. By keeping these numbers, you are becoming an effective manager of your own business-development program.

to the for-sale-by-owners or expired listings that you have contacted twice.

From your prospecting efforts, strive for the following results:

- Secure two showing appointments with qualified buyers.
- Sell one home.

Apply Sales Skills 6 and 7 (see Section 9) as you work with buyers and sellers this week. Refer to Sections 8 and 9 in this book for more information.

See Figure 7.4, *Joan's Fourth Week: 30 Days to Dollars.* It is your prototype prospecting plan; your plan should look similar.

Business Support

Refine and complete your listing process. Complete your entire listing process materials; include eight visuals to counter sellers' objections. Apply the AAA technique to objection-busters to use with your visuals.

Complete your personal promotion materials and plan. Complete your professional portfolio or personal brochure. Include a distribution plan for using these tools to promote yourself, to prospect, and to keep in touch with your customers and clients.

Complete and systematize your buyer process. Review and complete your buyers' counseling packet. Include eight visuals to counter buyers' common objections.

Continue your contact management data entry and follow-up plan.

Your Next Step

Congratulations! You have experienced your first four weeks in the business. Not only have you completed this program, you have formed the habits of successful self-management:

- Completing consistent, *high-number contacts* for prospects
- Qualifying prospects for time management and control of your career
- Applying *sales skills* to your sales cycle
- *Creating business-producing activities* in large numbers

FIGURE 7.4   Joan's Fourth Week: 30 Days to Dollars

Activity	Weekly Minimum
1. Contact people you know/meet.	
In-person calls	20
Phone calls	30
Follow-up (phone calls, mail, e-mail, etc.)	50

Joan contacts 50 people.

2. Circle prospect in person.	25

Joan circle prospects 25 homes.

3. Choose one additional activity from these.

Farm Area	in-person contacts	50
	or	
FSBOs	in-person or phone contacts	25
	or	
Expired listings	in-person or phone contacts	25

Joan calls on 25 FSBOs and 25 expireds.

4. Hold public open houses.	1

Joan holds 1 open house.

Total weekly minimum in-person/phone contacts: 100-125

You have organized the support systems to the business that allow you to move faster:

- *Listing process* systems
- *Market analysis* package
- Working knowledge of *purchase and sale agreements*
- System for *counseling/qualifying* buyers
- Follow-up and *contact management* system
- *Personal promotional* tools and plan

You have dramatically increased your sales skills. You have practiced and applied the Seven Critical Sales Skills to success, so that you can better help buyers and sellers.

Continue your business development plan, analyze it, make changes as needed and plan longer-term. To help you take your planning process to the next level, refer to my book, *The Real Estate Agent's Business Planning Guide,* listed in the Reference section. It shows you how to budget, explains marketing programs, gives you dozens of personal marketing ideas, and assists you as you become an experienced top producer.

Congratulations on completing a challenging yet rewarding system that will get you off to the start in your real estate career that you need to ensure success. Continue the habits that you have begun, and you will enjoy a high-producing, profitable, long-term career.

8

Getting Leads

To get your business off to a quick start, you will want to go to the best sources for *leads*. To create your prospecting plan, follow these four principles of real estate marketing:

1. Segment your markets.
2. Be proactive.
3. Work the best sources.
4. Work the numbers.

Segment Markets. The population explosion, information overload—these and other cultural developments make it impossible to promote yourself effectively to everyone. To be an effective prospector today, you must *segment and prioritize* your potential markets. By segmenting your potential markets, you will discover certain best *targets*. A *target market* is a group of people defined through common demographics (i.e., age, income, real estate needs) and psychographics (i.e., lifestyle). To be an effective marketer, you need to clearly define your target markets and devise specific methods to sell to each. *30 Days to Dollars* segments markets and prioritizes them by *best sources of business.*

Be Proactive.   To be successful in real estate today, you must get most of your business from *proactive prospecting*—you go out and meet people. *30 Days to Dollars* uses mainly proactive activities. There are two kinds of prospecting:

1. Proactive—you go out and find people
2. Reactive—you sit and wait for people

You can control the number of leads you can get (and the money you make) through proactive methods.

Work the Best Sources.   To be successful, you should start with your best sources of business. *30 Days to Dollars* prioritizes these sources for you. *Proactive sources* include:

- Best—people you know
- Good—circle prospecting
- Immediate sources of listings:

    —For-sale-by-owners (FSBOs)

    —Expired listings
- Long-term—geographical farm

Reactive sources include:

- Open houses
- Floor time (This is not covered in *30 Days to Dollars,* as your office probably schedules floor time for you. To develop the special sales communication skills required to secure appointments via the telephone, I suggest you take a role-play oriented workshop in telephone techniques.)

Work the Numbers.   To be an effective marketer, you must make enough calls to generate quality leads. *30 Days to Dollars* shows you which markets to target and how many calls you need to make—overall, 100 sales calls per week to ensure success—one sale and one listing in your first 30 days in the business.

Standard Methods for Getting Leads

This section shows you exactly how to make the sales call in each of the target markets in *30 Days to Dollars*.

There are literally thousands of ways to make sales calls and to follow up. The best way is the one that works for you. Start with one method, then make adjustments for your style and market area. *The best way is simply to get out into the field and start.*

As you learn to make these calls, you will practice and apply sales skills. These sales skills are referred to in your weekly assignments. The "how to" of these skills is found in Sections 8 and 9.

Practice makes perfect. Before you make a sales call, "craft" your sales approach, using the sales skills described on the following pages. Before you actually apply the sales skill in person, practice them with your manager, a fellow agent, or your spouse, friend, or child—they will provide valuable feedback to help you be more effective in your actual sales calls.

Best Sources of Business: People You Know

To *craft a sales call* (Sales Skill 1, to be applied in Week One), use the following technique:

- Think of a particular person to call.
- Determine a potential real estate need and *benefit* (Sales Skill 2, to be applied in Week One) to this person.
- To discover these needs, write three questions to ask the person.
- Determine your *call objective.*
- Write a *question to get a lead* (Sales Skill 3, to be applied in Week One) or appointment—meet your objective.
- Write an opening statement.

This method of crafting calls works for crafting any initial sales call. For example:

- Joe Smith is a family friend.
- A potential real estate need and benefit to Joe is a rental home, which will reduce his tax burden.

- Three questions to ask:
  1. Is the equity in your present home enough to get a second mortgage to refinance for money to buy another home?
  2. Have you thought about reducing your tax burden?
  3. Have you looked into purchasing a home as a rental?
- The *call objective* is to get an appointment.
- The question to get the appointment is: When can we explore this potential?
- The opening statement is: I have been thinking about you. I'm in real estate now, and I have been exploring how to help people ease financial burdens with real estate.

Advanced Techniques.   *Accept the first no, and have the next question ready.* With people you know, ask: Since I'm starting my real estate career, could I count on you to refer me to those who want to buy or sell? I'll touch base with you regularly.

Find a reason to keep in touch. With people you know, ask: Can I put you on my mailing list? We have a wonderful real estate newsletter that keeps you updated on the market, so that you will have the latest in specific real estate information.

Relationship Marketing Again

Remember the trend, "Relationship Marketing". You are not trying just to get a lead now. You are establishing yourself as a real estate professional. With someone you know, you have opportunities and barriers. The opportunity comes because the person already trusts you. The barrier is there because the person knows you "in another life"— so you must remove the barrier.

How will you prove to a person who, for example, knows you as a musician that you are now a capable real estate professional? Develop a distribution plan (a marketing plan over time) that reminds this person you are now practicing real estate successfully. Mailings to this person are easy. They are the same mailings you are doing to promote properties. Each time you have a brochure or flyer on a property you or someone in your office has listed, merely drop that flyer in the mail with a note: "Just wanted you to know the latest in property values," "Just wanted to keep you abreast of the market," "Thought this property would fit some of our friends," or "Please pass on this information to someone you know." By sending the flyer you are teaching your friend that you are actively engaged in selling real estate. You are also showing your friend, that, over time, you are accountable for keeping in touch in a professional way.

Ask yourself, "What barriers must I overcome to prove to my friends that I am a capable, trustworthy salesperson?" Of course, as a musician, a barrier I had to overcome was that I was this person who tickled the ivories and entertained people. Could this entertaining person be entrusted with thousands of dollars of my friend's money? Some of my friends didn't know me in any business world.

What I knew about myself, though, was that I had to have been dutiful, responsible and accountable to have practiced piano regularly all through college, and held a job requiring 12 hours of work a week, while still finding time to study. I knew I could handle several things at once—a skill certainly required in real estate. Also, I knew I had become a pretty good negotiator from having to negotiate fees for music jobs. What I needed to do was to demonstrate those same skills to my friends in a new business.

So that you know your strengths, you need to do an analysis of your skills, then demonstrate them through how you communicate with people you know. Create verbal asides that reinforce what you know are your strong points. You MUST remind your friends of your competencies, in a gracious way, through what you say and the messages you send. Otherwise, they won't get it. My observation is that I didn't get it about myself, and most agents don't get it. That is, we don't realize that the behaviors we demonstrated in our "former lives" are the same behaviors we will demonstrate in our real estate careers. People don't change.

Circle Prospecting: Positioning You with Real Estate Success

Circle prospecting means contacting homeowners in person to provide them with information about a property in their area. The object of circle prospecting is to get a lead.

You should use the circle prospect technique in the following situations

- A new listing
- A house sold
- A listing sold
- An open house

To use circle prospecting in personal promotion, include this strategy in your listing presentation as a service to sellers and promote yourself as you circle prospect. As a new agent, use this strategy to ask an agent in your office for the opportunity. You have literally 60 to 100 opportunities per month to circle prospect.

There are two important keys to success in circle prospecting:

1. Contact homeowners in person only.
2. Visit the same homeowner three times within a short period.

To prepare for circle prospecting, first decide on the reason why you are calling on the homeowner. Then create your materials, and design your script using the *craft a sales call* (Sales Skill 1) method:

- Introduce yourself, and tell the homeowner why you are there. Be sure to include a benefit (Sales Skill 2) to the homeowner.
- Ask the homeowner about the property: Have you seen it?
- *Ask for a lead* (Sales Skill 3): Do you know anyone who . . . ? (indirect) Are you thinking of . . . ? (direct)

Advanced Technique.   Design your script to have a second question ready to follow up the first "no" (see indirect and direct questions example above). Let's say that your first question is: Do you know anyone who . . . ? Your next question can be: Are you thinking of . . . ?

It Works

Circle prospecting works for several reasons:

- Homeowners are curious about what is happening in their area.
- Because few agents will take advantage of this opportunity, you have no competition with other agents!
- Homeowners want to see an agent face-to-face.

To increase your chances of a lead, try this advanced technique: Familiarity breeds trust—go back three times.

Other Methods for Finding Leads

In the *30 Days to Dollars* plan, three other proactive sources of leads are explained. Immediate sources of leads include: *for-sale-by-owners* (FSBOs) and *expired listings*. A long-term source of leads is *the geographical farm.*

To select the target markets that you will specialize in, first, assess your background and sales skills. Then assess your market area. Discuss your market area and your competition for these sources of business with your manager. Your manager is an excellent resource for you as you choose the best target markets on which to focus your efforts.

On the following pages are *contact methods* for developing leads from two of these sources. Because farming is a long-term method of finding leads, it is not included. (See REALTOR® *Magazine,* published by the National Association of REALTORS®, for excellent articles on farming.) These contact methods are by no means the only ones. Read materials in your office. Find agent specialists in each of these markets. Assemble your own "call program."

For-Sale-by-Owners

There are dozens of methods for calling on FSBOs. To contact and convert them, you must make this market a specialty and highly develop your sales approach. Here's an approach that works well for the new agent. Although it requires little developed sales skill, it does require consistency.

The Concept.   Surveys show that something happens to FSBOs within six weeks: Owners list their property, sell it themselves, or take it off the market. In your area, do a market survey to determine any differences in time frame for this process and adjust the strategy in Figure 8.1 accordingly.

When executing this program, remember the following important aspects:

- Make all sales calls in person.
- Follow up consistently.
- Give a new piece of information (not too much) each week.
- Ask if there is anything about the information you left the prior week that the seller needs help with.
- Don't give detailed information.

By Week Six the sellers will tire of trying to sell their home. When you ask about the information you provided the seller, make an appointment to explain the information while all sellers are present (a first listing appointment). Go to the appointment, and start your listing process.

FIGURE 8.1 Converting FSBOs

Call/Time Frame	What to Say	What to Give
When sign first goes up	Introduce yourself; mention saw sign; here are materials to help you; I'll be back	One piece of buying/selling information
Week 2	Same as above; ask question about materials given*	Same
Week 3	Same	Same
Week 4	Same	Same
Week 5	Same	Same
Week 6	Same	Same

*This question is key to this system.

Success Rate.   Using this program, *you can convert one out of five sellers.*

Expired Listings

These sellers want to sell. Your challenge is the dissatisfied customer. Because the home did not sell, the agent who had listed the home has created a high level of customer dissatisfaction. This objection isn't just with that agent and company—it's with all real estate companies. To call on expired listings, you must make this a *specialty* and carefully *plan your strategy.*

You can use any number of ways to contact expired listings. Here are the steps to designing a system:

• Read articles, and find agent specialists in these areas.

- Design your method relative to your market, company, and personal style.
- Make the sales calls.
- Make adjustments to your method.

Find the listings that have just expired in your area. Target those that you think will sell if you can get a price reduction. Following is one method successful agents have used to call on expired listings.

Prepare a Script. Hello. I'm Josie Smith of ABC Realty. Is your home still on the market? (If no . . .) Are you still interested in selling it? (If yes . . .) I have some information concerning your home that will be useful to you—whenever or if you decide to put your home back on the market. I assure you I won't ask for a listing now. After all, I don't even know if I could help you until I do some research (e.g., see the home, do a market analysis).

May I come by and drop off this information? (Seller will probably ask you why.) It's in all sellers' best interests to move properties, whether real estate agents list and sell the property or not. I want to assist you in your marketing efforts. Hopefully, if in the future you should decide to market your home with a real estate professional, you will feel comfortable enough with me and my service that you will think of me.

Information to Take with You

You want to demonstrate your ability to provide expert information and service that the sellers need to market their property successfully. You should include information in your area about changing market trends, helpful hints to selling, and information on why now is the right time to buy.

At the Appointment. Use Sales Skill 5, the "hum" technique, to probe for more illuminating information. Ask these questions:

- So I better understand the specifics of your home, do you mind if I ask you some questions?
- When you sold a home before (if they did), what was the best marketing strategy the agent used?
- In your opinion, why hasn't your home sold?
- If you were to list again, what would you be looking for in a real estate agent?

- Where are you moving to? How soon must you be there?

When you find an area of the seller's need, fill that need with a benefit of your service to the seller. Close for a listing presentation appointment.

Advanced Technique.   Go for it! Toward the end of your conversation, when appropriate, ask: What would it take for you to list with me?

9

Seven Critical Sales Skills for Success

Yes, you can sell homes to people without having effective sales skills. However, it's much more enjoyable for everyone involved if you are a skilled sales communicator. Many buyers have been discouraged from purchasing a home because the salesperson was unskilled at helping the buyer make a buying decision!

Seven Critical Sales Skills

Learning the Seven Critical Sales Skills will help you develop masterful communication skills that will be useful in any sales situation. Take time to develop these skills. Use them in all sales situations until you're at ease with them. The following skills will save you time, create better relationships, and make you more money:

1. *Craft a sales call script.* To get the "biggest bang" from your sales call, always aim for a lead. Refer to "Craft a Sales Call" in Section 8 and on the following page for suggestions on how to call on people you know. This same crafting method can be used in designing any sales call. This sales skill is practiced and applied in Week One.

2. *Attach benefits.* Show customers that there is something in it for them. Too often, salespeople only think of what a sale will do for them, not what it will provide for the buyers of their services! This sales skill is practiced and applied in Week One. (See page 137 for more information on how to attach benefits.)

3. *Ask a question to get the order.* This sales skill is introduced in Section 8, when you're crafting a sales call to a person you know and when you're circle prospecting. It seems simplistic, but too often salespeople fail to ask for the order. To ensure that you get a lead, craft and apply this simple yet critical sales skill in all sales situations. This sale skill is introduced in Week One and is demonstrated on the audiotape. (See page 138 for more information on how to ask for a lead.

4. *Use the AAA method of objection-busting.* This method of crafting a process to counter, defuse or anticipate objections is critical to each sales situation. In truth, all salespeople encounter objections and rejections with each sales call. With the AAA method, you learn to craft a whole process that takes objections from an adversary relationship to a discussion. Use this method, introduced in Week Two, to qualify buyers and sellers, and throughout the entire sales cycle. (See page 138 for information on crafting an objection-buster using the AAA method.)

5. *Use the "hum" technique.* This technique is a simplified version of asking questions that encourage the buyer of your services to open up (in sales, these are called *open-ended questions*). This method also helps you get in-depth infor-

mation so that you understand your buyer's needs (in sales, this is called *probing*.) Use this technique, introduced in Week Three.

6. *Tie down your benefit statement.* Sometimes agents get enamored with the sound of their own sales voices. The "tie-down" brings the buyer of your services back into the conversation, and allows you to check to be sure you are still on track. This sales skill is introduced in Week Four. Use it throughout the sales cycle to ensure that the buyer of your services is still buying what you have to sell. (See the information on page 141 about how to craft a "tie down.")

7. *Discover the motive that drives the buyers' decisions.* People make decisions based on feelings and rationalize these decisions with facts. For example, let's say your friend buys a Mercedes. Does he say that he bought it because he wants status? No. He says he bought it as studies show the car will actually cost less in the long run because it will hold its value. While this may be true, your friend's desire for status prompted his decision. (Emotions drive decisions.)

Using this sales skill, you can discover the dominant motive of the buyer of services. Then, you can create a meaningful sales cycle to appeal to that particular buyer of services. To close, you remind the buyer of his or her motive. This sales skill is introduced in Week Four. Use it throughout the sales cycle to help the buyer of services motivate himself or herself to make a good buying decision. (See the information on page 141 about how to discover the "dominant buying motive.")

Sales Skill 1: Craft a Sales Call

The following method of crafting calls works for crafting any initial sales call. As this is a prospecting method and a sales skill, it is included in Sections 8 and 9. Use the worksheet in Figure 9.1 to craft a sales call. Here's the process:

- Think of a particular person to call.

- Determine potential real estate needs and *benefits* to this person that you can provide.

- To discover these needs, write three questions to ask this person.

- Determine your *call objective.*

FIGURE 9.1   Craft Your Own Sales Call

Name of person:_____

Potential real estate need:_____

Benefit to the person of
your service:_____

Three questions:

    1 ._____

    2._____

    3._____

Your call objective:_____

Question to get the order:_____

Opening statement:_____

Practice this sales call with a friend until you are comfortable.

- Write a question to *get a lead* or appointment—meet your objective.
- Write an opening statement.

Example

- The person: Joe Smith, a friend of your family.
- A potential real estate need and benefit to Joe is a rental home, which will reduce his tax burden.
- Three questions to ask:
  1. Is the equity in your present home enough to secure a second mortgage to refinance for money to buy another home?
  2. Have you considered reducing your tax burden?
  3. Have you looked into purchasing a home as a rental?

- The call objective is to get an appointment.
- The question to get an appointment: When can we explore this potential?
- The opening statement is: I've been thinking about you. I'm in real estate now. I'm exploring how to help people ease financial burdens with real estate.

Sales Skill 2: Attach a Benefit

A *benefit* is a statement to the buyer of your services that answers the question in the buyer's mind: What does it mean to me?

Too often a salesperson recites the facts (called *features* in sales), thinking that, if those facts are important to the salesperson, they must be important to the buyer. Unfortunately, this is not generally the case. What is important and interesting to the buyer is how he or she can use these facts. A three-car garage is a benefit to the person who owns three cars (or lots of things). It's merely an unwanted expense to a single person with one car!

How do you discover what is important to a buyer? When a buyer requests a specific feature or need (e.g., a large family room), ask *why?* Then, when you show a home with a large family room, remind the buyer that it provides plenty of space for that growing family. In this way, the buyer sees the relevance of the large family room.

Following is an example of a benefit-attached statement: The home has a *two-car garage* (feature), so that *you can park your two full-sized cars there* (benefit). Benefits answer the buyer's question: So what? To attach benefits to features, state the feature first. Then, "bridge" to the benefit with the words "so that . . . "

Practice attaching benefits to the following features:

Feature	Bridge	Benefit
Family room . . .	so that	
Fireplace . . .	so that	
Low house payments . . .	so that	

Referrals to the agent are a benefit to the referring source because . . .

Listing with me is a benefit to you, the seller, because . . .

Working with me to find a home is a benefit to you, the buyer, because . . .

Sales Skill 3: Ask a Question To Get the Order

An order is a lead, a buying decision, a "yes" of any type. Usually, an order is given to an agent in reply to a question asked by the agent.

Do buyers give REALTORS® leads without being asked? It depends on the level of trust and rapport between agent and buyer.

Always ask a question to get an order. In this overcommunicated world, it's hard for any of us to find the energy to ask the salesperson to sell us something! Also, with a big-ticket item like a home, buyers may be less apt to do the salesperson's work! You should always ask a question to get an order. Successful salespeople always ask; less successful salespeople are afraid to ask—and may miss golden opportunities to increase their businesses.

Many agents expect customers to tell the agent that they want to buy a property. So, the agent waits for the customers to give an indication that they are ready to buy. In most cases, customers will not ask to buy. Once in a while, they will.

Asking for a Specific Order—A Lead

To get a lead, attach a benefit to your question. For example: Well, Sally, I appreciate your telling me that you would help me get started in real estate. When you give me names of people who want to buy or sell real estate, you'll be helping your friends get the very best service available (benefit). The only way to become proficient at asking for leads is to practice.

Getting Leads When Knocking on Doors

When knocking on doors, you can phrase a question two ways:

1. *Direct question:* Are you thinking of selling/buying?
2. *Indirect question:* Do you know of anyone who is thinking of buying/selling?

Sales Skill 4: Use the AAA Method of Objection-Busting

Just think of objections as one of the six "no's" that you need to accept from your buyer to get to "yes."

To craft an objection-buster gracefully, use the AAA method:

- Agree
- Ask
- Answer

When the objection comes from the buyer (the buyer of your services, whether a purchaser or seller), **agree** that he or she has an important point. After all, it's important to the buyer! Instead of countering the objection and risking an argument, **ask** more questions to discover just exactly what the buyer is talking about. **Answer** the objection with new information. Then, close!

The dialogue would go something like this:

Buyer: I want to wait to purchase. (objection)

You agree: I understand your concern. Buying is a big decision.

You ask: To help me understand exactly what you're thinking about, do you mind if I ask you a few questions?

You probe and ask more: Tell me more about waiting to purchase.

You provide an answer: There's some information that could help you make the best decision. Let me show you. . . . Do you have any questions? Let's go ahead.

Use the worksheet, Crafting an Objection-Buster (see Figure 9.2), to create an objection-buster for each of the objections you are working on in *Up and Running*.

Sales Skill 5: The "Hum" Technique

Often agents assume that they know what buyers mean by the words they use and jump ahead, many times missing important clues. For example, a buyer says he wants a *deal*. You assume you know what *deal* means to the buyer, and you show him homes that may not be deals to the buyer.

To avoid jumping to conclusions, use the *hum technique*. This skill, a simplified version of the question-and-probing sales skill, is fun to use. It provides lots of information and encourages the buyer to keep talking.

Here's the technique:

* Ask an open-ended question (one that requires more of an answer than yes or no). Hint: Open-ended questions are those that start with who, what, when, where, how much, why.
* Listen to the answer, pick out a core word, and repeat the word back to the talker, using a questioning upswing to your word. This will encourage your questioner to tell you more.
* As your talker talks, simply *hum*. This, too, will encourage the buyer to continue talking. You'll discover lots of information and show that you are a skilled, attentive listener.

FIGURE 9.2   Crafting an Objection-Buster

Objection

You **Agree**_____

You **Ask** _____

More Probing Questions

(Tell me more.)_____

(Please explain.)_____

(Then what happened.)_____

(How, what, when, why, how much.)_____

_____

You **Answer**

(Use visuals.)_____

_____

_____

Close

_____

_____

_____

_____

The dialogue would go something like this:

Buyer says: I want a deal.

You ask: Deal?

Buyer explains. You hum, encouraging the buyer to give you more information. Alternate saying key words with hums.

When To Use This Sales Skill

Use this skill all the time. Successful salespeople aren't good talkers; they're good listeners. See how long you can continue a conversation without actually saying a whole sentence. When you can talk with someone for three minutes and let them do all the talking, you're on your way to becoming an effective salesperson.

Sales Skill 6: Tie Down Your Benefit

This is another simple sales skill, but one that's very important for creating rapport, agreement and movement toward closing. To use this technique, attach a question to your benefit statement. This ties down the benefit in your customer's mind. It relates the benefit to the buyer.

For example: This home has a three-car garage, which allows you to keep your antique cars at home, saving you rent. *That is what you want, isn't it?*

Practice tie-downs using the worksheet in Figure 8.3.

Sales Skill 7: Discover the Motive That Drives the Decision

As a salesperson, you need to have an attitude like Detective Colombo. Always wearing an old raincoat, Colombo spent his time trying to discover people's motives for the crimes he investigated. Without a motive, Colombo couldn't figure out who did it.

What are motives? They are emotional reasons that people take actions. People buy homes to fill emotional needs—motives. Three bathrooms are not very motivating; however, providing space for a growing family is. To find motives, attach benefits to features. Benefits lead to dominant buying motives, the main emotional reasons behind people make buying decisions. Buying motives include:

- Personal space
- Prestige
- Security
- Family security

FIGURE 9.3   Practice Tie-Downs

Feature	Bridge	Benefit	Tie-down question
Large lot	so that . . .	you can have . . .	That's what you want, isn't it?
Private setting			
Quiet street			
Low down payment			

One motive always dominates the others. People often do not know their own dominant buying motives, but they can express their needs in terms of features. They can agree on benefits. You need to help them translate their physical needs to emotional needs.

You can identify which needs people are trying to fill by the benefits they want to have as they buy or sell. For example: "I want a nice home for my family, on a safe cul-de-sac." The dominant buying motive is obviously family security.

Why did you buy your last home? Identify *your* own emotional needs. Your success in selling homes to people depends on your ability to discover dominant buying motives and to remind buyers of these motives as you work with and ask them closing questions. Your success in listing homes at the right price depends on your ability to help identify sellers' dominant buying motives, to help them motivate themselves to sell.

When you're sleuthing for dominant buying motives, use the worksheet shown in Figure 9.4.

FIGURE 9.4   Dominant Buying Motives

Features They Want	Benefits to Them	Dominant Buying Motive

Sellers and Buyers

FIGURE 10.1   For Sellers: Qualified Listing Appointments

Date of Presentation	Name	Address	Want To Sell Both Home	2 Hours Pre-Scheduled	How Much $ Want	Marketing Presentation Completed	Results

---

FIGURE 10.2   Evaluate Property Salability

---

1. Property listed at competitive price.   Yes_____   No_____

2. Full-term listing agreement.   Yes_____   No_____

3. Seller to complete obvious repairs/cleaning
    prior to showing.   Yes_____   No_____

4. Easy access (e.g., key, phone for showing).   Yes_____   No_____

5. Yard sign.   Yes_____   No_____

6. Immediate possession.   Yes_____   No_____

7. Extras included (e.g., appliances).   Yes_____   No_____

8. Available for first tour.   Yes_____   No_____

9. Government terms available.   Yes_____   No_____

10. Owner financing available.   Yes_____   No_____

11. Below market down payment.   Yes_____   No_____

12. Below market interest rate.   Yes_____   No_____

13. Post-dated price reduction.   Yes_____   No_____

14. Market commission.   Yes_____   No_____

15. In my evaluation, this property will sell within
    listed market range, in normal market time
    for this area.   Yes_____   No_____

16. My credibility as a professional will be
    enhanced by listing this property.   Yes_____   No_____

FIGURE 10.3   Qualified Buyers

Date of Qualify Meeting	Name	Address	Qualify Checklist Used	Both @ Qualifying Session	# Showings	Sales

FIGURE 10.4 **Evaluate Your Customer's Potential**

Rate on a scale of 1–4 (4 being the highest)

1. Customer is motivated to purchase.
   (Rate each spouse/partner separately.)   1   2   3   4

2. Customer is realistic about price range expectations.   1   2   3   4

3. Customer is open and cooperative.   1   2   3   4

4. Customer will purchase in a timely manner.   1   2   3   4

5. Customer is a referral source and will provide referrals.   1   2   3   4

6. Customer has agreed that you will be his or her
   exclusive agent.   1   2   3   4

7. Agent has established a positive rapport with
   customer.   1   2   3   4

8. Customer will meet with loan officer.   1   2   3   4

9. Customer answered financial questions openly.   1   2   3   4

10. Customer has no other agent obligations.   1   2   3   4

11. If customer has home to sell, he or she is realistic
    about price.   1   2   3   4

12. Customer will devote sufficient time to purchasing
    process.   1   2   3   4

13. Both spouses/partners will be available to look for home.   1   2   3   4

Is this customer worthy of your time, energy, and expertise?

Walking Through
a Sample Business Plan

FIGURE 11.1   Joan's Yearly Goals Translated to Monthly Goals and Activities

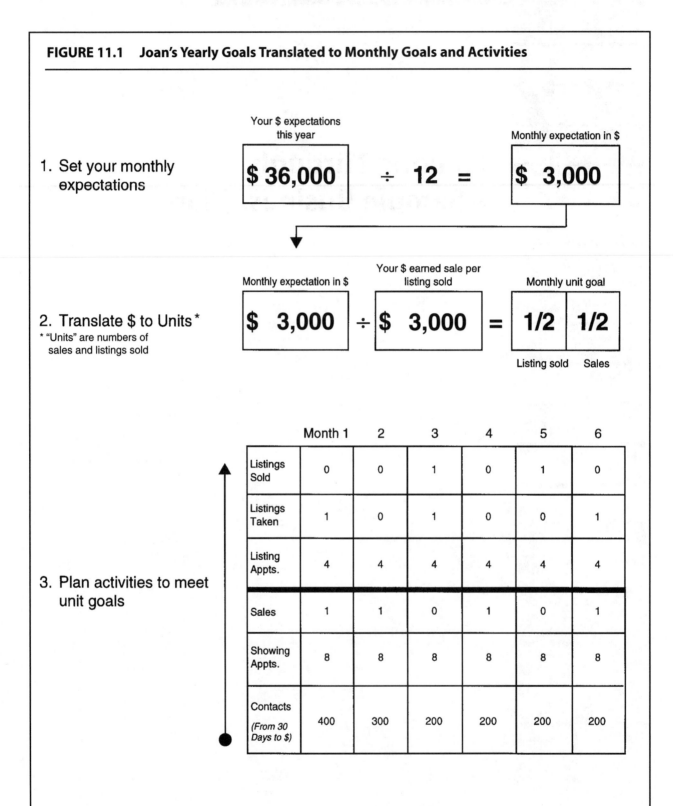

FIGURE 11.2   Joan's Plan: From Breakeven to Profitability

1. Estimate your activities and when they will create income. Start with face-to-face contacts.

Activity / Income	1	2	3	4	5	6	7	8	9	10	11	12	Totals
Closings *			1	1		1							
Sales *	1	1		1		1							
Listings sold *					1	1							
Listings secured	1		1		1	1							
Showings	8	8	8	8	8	8							
Listing presentations	4	4	4	4	4	4							
Face-to-face contacts	400	300	200	200	200	200							

*Each unit is worth $3,000 in commissions earned or paid.

2. Tally your expenses per month. Log in your projected earnings and "paids."

	1	2	3	4	5	6	7	8	9	10	11	12	Totals
Business expenses†	1,149	748	818	748	888	818							
Earned income†	3,000	3,000	0	3,000	3,000	6,000							
Paid income	0	0	3,000	3,000	0	3,000							
Profit per month	-$1,149	-$748	$2,182	$2,252	-$888	$2,182							

†See *The Real Estate Agent's Business Planning Guide* for a detailed listing of expenses and budgeting.

FIGURE 11.3   Joan's First Week: 30 Days to Dollars

Activity	Weekly Minimum
1. Contact people you know/meet.	
In-person calls	20
Phone calls	30
Follow-up (mailers sent)	50
Joan contacts 50 people.	
2. Circle prospect in person.	25
Joan circle prospects 25 homes.	
3. Choose one additional activity from these.	
Farm Area in-person contacts	50
or	
FSBOs in-person or phone contacts	25
or	
Expired listings in-person or phone contacts	25
4. Hold public open houses.	1
Joan holds 1 open house.	

Total weekly minimum in-person/phone contacts: **100-125**

FIGURE 11.4   Joan's Second Week: 30 Days to Dollars

Activity	Weekly Minimum
1. Contact people you know/meet.	
In-person calls	20
Phone calls	30
Follow-up (mailers sent)	50

Joan contacts 50 people.

2. Circle prospect in person.	25

Joan circle prospects 25 homes.

3. Choose one additional activity from these.

Farm Area	in-person contacts	50
	or	
FSBOs	in-person or phone contacts	25
	or	
Expired listings	in-person or phone contacts	25

Joan calls on 25 expired listings.

4. Hold public open houses.	1

Joan holds 1 open house.

Total weekly minimum in-person/phone contacts: **100-125**

FIGURE 11.5   Joan's Third Week: 30 Days to Dollars

Activity	Weekly Minimum
1. Contact people you know/meet.	
In-person calls	20
Phone calls	30
Follow-up (mailers sent)	50
Joan contacts 50 people.	
2. Circle prospect in person.	25
Joan circle prospects 25 homes.	
3. Choose one additional activity from these.	
Farm Area in-person contacts	50
or	
FSBOs in-person or phone contacts	25
or	
Expired listings in-person or phone contacts	25
Joan calls on 25 expired listings.	
4. Hold public open houses.	1
Joan holds 1 open house.	

Total weekly minimum in-person/phone contacts: **100–125**

FIGURE 11.6   Joan's Fourth Week: 30 Days to Dollars

Activity	Weekly Minimum
1. Contact people you know/meet.	
In-person calls	20
Phone calls	30
Follow-up (phone calls, mail, e-mail, etc.)	50

Joan contacts 50 people.

2. Circle prospect in person.	25

Joan circle prospects 25 homes.

3. Choose one additional activity from these.

Farm Area	in-person contacts	50
	or	
FSBOs	in-person or phone contacts	25
	or	
Expired listings	in-person or phone contacts	25

Joan calls on 25 FSBOs and 25 expireds.

4. Hold public open houses.	1

Joan holds 1 open house.

Total weekly minimum in-person/phone contacts: **100-125**

FIGURE 11.7   Joan's 30 Days to Dollars Plan (Prospecting)

Month: _____

Proactive Activities	Week 1		Week 2		Week 3		Week 4		Totals	
	G	A	G	A	G	A	G	A	G	A
People you know/meet [50/week]	50	50	50	50	50	50	50	50	200	200
Circle prospect [25/week]	25	25	25	25	25	25	25	25	100	100
Farm [50/week]	0	0	0	0	0	0	0	0	0	0
FSBOs [25/week]	0	0	0	0	25	25	25	25	50	50
Expireds [25/week]	0	0	25	25	25	25	25	25	75	75
Reactive Activities										
Open houses [1min]	1	1	1	1	1	1	1	1	4	4

FIGURE 11.8　Joan's Monthly Activity Scorecard

Month: _____

Buyer Activities

	Week 1		Week 2		Week 3		Week 4		Totals	
	G	A	G	A	G	A	G	A	G	A
Counseling Appointments w/ buyers	2	2	2	2	2	2	2	2	8	8
Qualified buyer showings	2	2	2	2	2	2	2	2	8	8
# sales							1	1	1	1

Listing Activities

	Week 1		Week 2		Week 3		Week 4		Totals	
	G	A	G	A	G	A	G	A	G	A
Qualified listing appointments	1	1	1	1	1	1	1	1	4	4
Marketable listings secured	0	0	0	0	1	1	0	0	1	1
# of listings sold	0	0	0	0	0	0	0	0	0	0

FIGURE 11.9   Joan's Weekly Plan

Name: Joan Smith

Week: One

Time	Monday	Tuesday	Wednesday	Thursday	Friday	Saturday	Sunday
7–8	Organize desk		Day off	Write 40 follow-up cards			
8–9	Office meeting	Paperwork			Meet w/mgr	Paperwork	
9–10	Office tour →	Call 20 people I know		Call 10 people to ask for leads →	Call 20 people to ask for leads →	Show homes	Show homes
10–11	→	→		→	→	→	→
11–12		Floor time		Paperwork	Inspect		Lunch
12–1	Office orient.	Lunch		Lunch	Lunch	Lunch	Follow-up
1–2	Inspect inventory	Start market analysis		Inspect inventory	Inspect	Floor time	
2–3	→	→		→	Continue mkt. analysis	→	Visits
3–4	Call people I know	Follow-up		Follow-up	→	Inspect inventory	
4–5	List 100 people to ask for leads	Inspect inventory		Meet with loan officer	Circle prospect 25 homes	Circle prospect 25 homes	
5–6	→	→	→	→	→	→	→
6–7							
7–8							Do listing presentation
8–9							→

SECTION

12

Forms to Create Your Own Plan

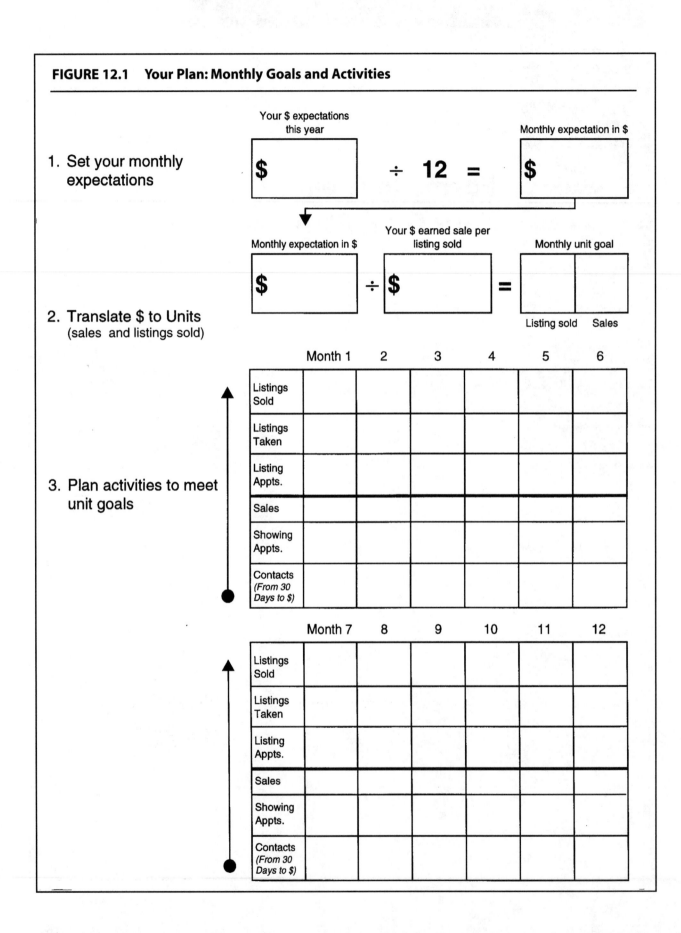

FIGURE 12.1   Your Plan: Monthly Goals and Activities

FIGURE 12.2   30 Days to Dollars

Activity	Weekly Minimum
1. Contact people you know/meet.	
In-person calls	20
Phone calls	30
Follow-up (phone calls, mail, e-mail, etc.)	50
2. Circle prospect in person.	25
3. Choose one additional activity from these.	
Farm Area in-person contacts	50
or	
FSBOs in-person or phone contacts	25
or	
Expired listings in-person or phone contacts	25
4. Hold public open houses.	1

Total weekly minimum in-person/phone contacts: **100-125**

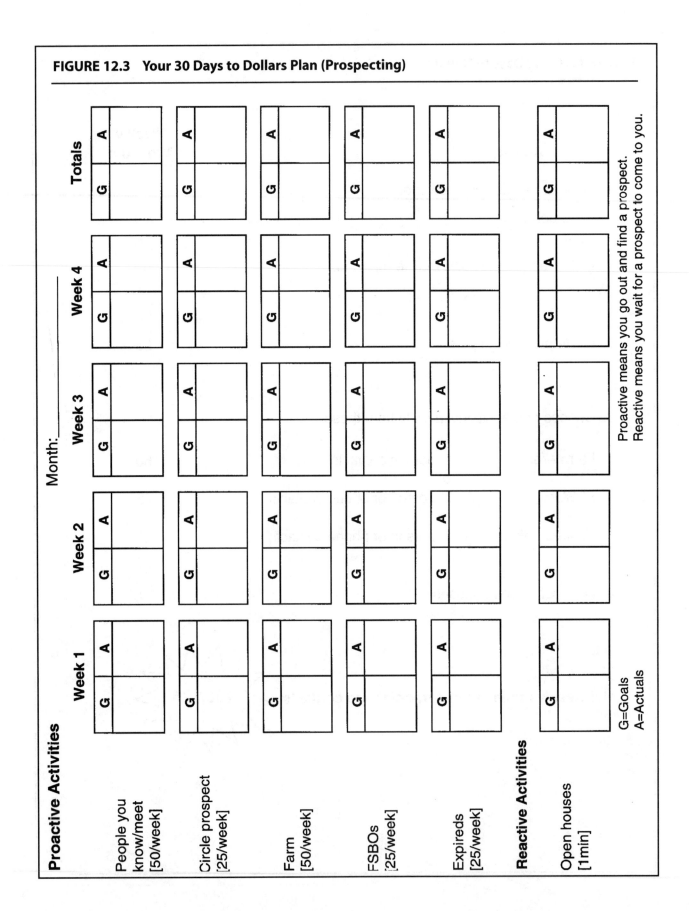

FIGURE 12.3   **Your 30 Days to Dollars Plan (Prospecting)**

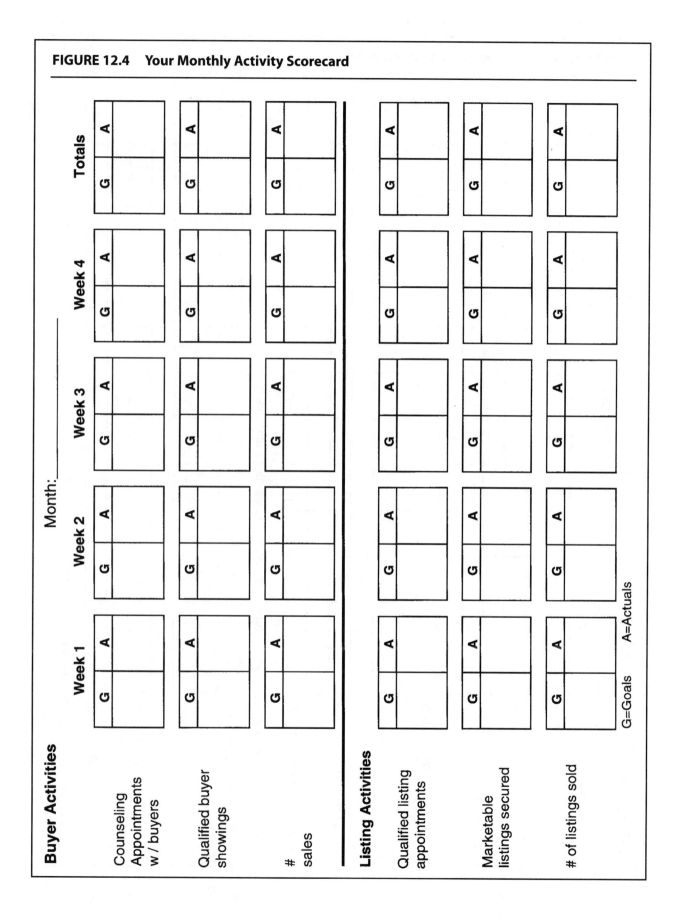

FIGURE 12.4 Your Monthly Activity Scorecard

FIGURE 12.5 From Breakeven to Profitability

1. Estimate your activities and when they will create income. Start with face-to-face contacts.

Activity / Income	1	2	3	4	5	6	7	8	9	10	11	12	Totals
Closings													
Sales													
Listings sold													
Listings secured													
Showings													
Listing presentations													
Face-to-face contacts													

Month

2. Tally your expenses per month. Log in your projected earnings and "paids."

Business Expenses													
Earned income													
Paid income													

Profit per month													

REFERENCES

Reaching Your Career Objectives

The Client-Based Marketing System. Carla Cross. Issaquah, WA: Carla Cross Seminars, Inc., 2001. The complete process for qualifying, listing, and marketing to sellers and sellers' properties. A fresh, contemporary "client-focused" approach to create client relationships and referrals for life, with 100-page handbook, audiotapes, and forms on disk.

The Complete Buyer's Agent Kit. Carla Cross and Herb Holcombe. Issaquah, WA: Carla Cross Seminars, Inc. 2001. (Co-author is the founder of the HomeBuyers' Network, a multi-million dollar producer with a team that specializes in representing first-time buyers only). A guide to "listing" buyers as effectively as listing sellers. All the presentation materials to create an effective pre-first visit presentation and a competitive buyers' presentation.

The Hottest e-Careers in Real Estate. Blanche Evans. Chicago: Dearborn™ Real Estate Education. 2000. Prominent real estate e-publisher, Blanche Evans, shares her know-how and advice on using the Internet to utmost effectiveness, then details seven new, yet proven e-careers ranging from buyer's agents and virtual brokers to commercial brokers and relocation specialists.

How about a Career in Real Estate? 2nd edition. Carla Cross. Issaquah, WA: Noteworthy Publishing. 1997. Endorsed and recommended by the Real Estate Brokerage Managers' Council of the National Association of REALTORS®. For prospective or new agents. Used by managers in recruiting, to explain real estate sales. Includes new agent expectations survey, real estate trends, activity schedules and budgeting.

On Track to Success in 30 Days. Carla Cross. Chicago: Dearborn™ Real Estate Education. 1996. The experienced agent's analytical tool to assess strengths and business challenges and move to a higher income level. Includes dozens of buyers' and sellers' strategy checklists, assessments, and systems. Used by managers to consult agents to higher production. Audiotapes demonstrating the skills available through Carla Cross Seminars, Inc.

The Real Estate Agent's Business Planning Guide. Carla Cross. Chicago: Dearborn™ Real Estate Education. 1994. Endorsed and recommended by Real Estate Brokerage Managers' Council of the National Association of REALTORS®. Audiotapes for agents and managers available through Carla Cross Seminars, Inc.

Terri Murphy's e-Listing and e-Selling Secrets for the Technologically Clueless. Terri Murphy. Chicago: Dearborn™ Real Estate Education, 2000. Real estate agents discover how to master the Internet to build an online presence, to prospect, to meet tech-savvy customers at their level, and most of all, to prosper in their real estate careers.

Your Professional Portfolio. Carla Cross. Issaquah, WA: Carla Cross Seminars, Inc. 2001. How to create a personal marketing book to promote yourself to buyers and sellers effectively. Use for open houses, qualifying interviews, to create loyalty in buyers and sellers. Includes resource book, examples, and disk for quick customization. Audiotapes provide explanation and role plays.

Assistance for Managers, Trainers, and Mentors

Advantage. Carla Cross. Issaquah, WA: Carla Cross Seminars, Inc. 1999. In-office complete new agent training system, from initial immediate activity checklist to business start-up plan to results-based training. A "plug and play system" for managers who are too busy to train. Includes eight modules, eight facilitator audiotapes, complete administrator systems, facilitator teaching guide, three student guides and student audiotapes in initial package.

The Conative Connection: Acting on Instinct. Kathy Kolbe. Addison-Wesley Publishing Co., a division of Pearson Education. 1997. Author explores the ways different personalities get into action.

"Crosscoaching": A Proven Mentor Program. Carla Cross. Issaquah, WA: Carla Cross Seminars, Inc. 1995. Critical points for effective mentor programs. Specific mentor and new agent guides, how to train/manage mentors. Detailed, ready to use, field-tested and proven. Includes audiotapes.

INDEX

A

Accomplishments, 41
  week one, 71
  week two, 86
  week three, 102
  week four, 118
Accountability, 3, 41
Action
  focus training, 4
  getting into, 91
  taking, 92
Action-focused training, 6
Activity
  plan, 11
  rewards of high, 25
  scorecard, 22, 24
Adaptation, 30
Advisor, 92
Agency
  disclosure, 89
  law, xv
Agent
  appointments, 41
  attitude of, xiv
  expectations, xi
Agree, 139
Answer, 139
Appointment, expired listing,
    131–32
Appraisals, xv
Ask, 139
Assignments, 40
Attitude
  challenge and, 35, 37
  changing, 37
  conscious control of, 40
  evaluating, 38–39
  management, 34–35, 38, 39
  shifts in, 37–38

B

Behaviors, 35, 37
Belief, 38, 39

Benefit attachment, 134, 137
Boundary establishment, 51–52
Breakeven to profitability, 26,
    28, 29–30, 153, 166
Brochure development, 104, 119,
    121
Budgets, 6
Business creation, 8
Business cycle, 12–13
Business development, xiii, xv,
    xvi, 11, 59–60
  activities, xviii, 13–14, 43
  business cycle and, 12–13
  business path, 13, 14
  prospecting, 16–22
  sales calls, 104
  sample, 25–30
  week one, 61, 70
  week two, 77–92
  week three, 93–108
  week four, 110, 119
Business management, 8
Business path, 13, 14, 31
Business plan
  creation of, xix–xx, 6
  earning power and, 33–34
  identifying pool, xvii
  success habits, xix
Business start-up plan, xix
  activities without one,
      xvii–xviii
  company selection and, 4
  effective, xviii
Business support, 59–60, 87, 89
  activities, xviii, 14, 43
  week one, 70–73
  week two, 78
  week three, 94, 104
  week four, 119
Buyer
  activities, 159, 165
  closing, selling, xii
  loyalty of, 89
  motivation, 135, 141–43

process, 119
Buying process, 89

C

Calls
  objective of, 126, 136
  working the numbers, 124
Challenge, 35, 37
Checklists, 5
Circle prospecting, 70, 127–28
Closing, xviii
  process, xv
  techniques, xvii, 58
Coach, xiii, xvi
  training of, 9
Coaching, 3, 41–43
  choosing, 9–10
  defined, 9
Cold calling, 17
Cold calling script, 17
Commission
  selecting company for, 4
  sliding scale, 10
  splits, 33
Communication, 13, 44–47
Companies, types of, 2–3
Company fit, 4
Company training program,
    xiv–xvi
Conclusions, 37, 39
Confidence, 74
Consultants, 40
Contact follow up, 126
Contact letters, 20
Contact management
  data entry, follow up, 119,
      121
  program, 5, 61, 70
  system, 89
Contact methods, 129, 130
Conversation control, 45–46
Conversion ratios, 56

Counseling buyers,121
Customer contact, 6

D

Daily plan, 43, 61
Daily planner, 64–69, 80–85
    week three, 96–101
    week four, 112–17
Database organization, 5
Deal, 140–41
Dependency, 33
Dependent real estate company, 2
Desk fee, 3
Digital camera, 6
Direction, 9
Distance learning, 6, 8
Distribution plan, 6, 70, 126
Dollar productive activities. See
    Business development activities
Downsizing, 7

E

E-company, 2
Education, xiv, xv, 7
Embarrassment, 91–92
Expectations, 41
Experience, 37, 91–92
Expired listings, 130–31

F

Floor time, 33, 73, 124
Flyers, 6, 126–27
Follow-through, xiii
Follow-up plan/program, 5, 89,
    104
For-sale-by-owner, 129–30
    conversion, 136
Franz, Rick, 12, 13

G

Game plan, 9, 41, 42
Geographical farm, 128
Goals, xvi, 35, 87, 152
Graduate-level courses, 8

H

Habits of failure, xvii
Handbook, 9
Hum technique, 104, 131,
    134–35, 139, 141

I

Independent business, 3, 34
Inspections, xv
Insurance plan, 22
Interdependent business, 3–4, 34
Internet, 2, 8, 20
Interview process, 35

J

Job description, 35, 36, 105

K

Knowledge, 105
Kolbe, Kathy, 91

L

Lead, 61, 70
    asking for, 70, 128, 138
    cost of, 33
    finding, 128–32
    knocking on doors, 138
    procurement, 10
    providing, 6
    segment markets, 123–24
    standard methods for, 125–28
Listening, 44–45, 47–48
Listing activities, 25, 26, 159,
    165
Listing agreements, xv
Listing appointments, 49, 50
    qualified, 146
Listing packages, 41
Listing process, 87, 119, 121

M

Mailing services, 19
Manager, 92
    agent appointments, 41
    guidance from 32–33
    helping agents, 40–41
    meeting with, 43
    perspective of, xiv
    role of, 40
Manager-agent success agree-
    ment, 41, 42
Market analysis, 121
Marketing plan, 51
Memorization, xvii
Mentoring, 9, 92
Mind, retraining, 39

Monetary goals, 27, 30
Monthly activity scorecard
    Joan's, 159
    yours, 165
Monthly goals
    Joan's, 152
    your, 162
Motivation, xiv, 38, 75, 92

N

National Association of
    REALTORS,® 129

O

Objection busting, 87, 89, 134,
    138–39, 140
Open house, 33, 73, 87, 107,
    124
Organization, xvii, 5
    technology and, 5–6
Organized activities schedule,
    xviii
Orientation checklist, 70
Orvis, Brian, 13
Overpriced homes, 51–52

P

Pacific Institute, 106
Partnership, 3, 41
People profiles, xi–xii
Personal digital assistant, 6, 61
Pictures, digital, 6
Plan of action, xii–xiii
Pocket personal computer, 61
Portfolio development, 104,
    107–8, 119, 121
Postcards, 19
Practicing perfectly, xv, 74–75,
    91, 106
Presenting/showing, xviii
Previewing properties, xii, xiii,
    xvii
Prioritizing activities, 13–14, 16
    business-supporting, xviii
    prototype schedule, 15
Priority list, 6
Proactive activities, 124, 158,
    164
Probing, 134–35
Professionalism, 48–49

Professionalism, projection of, 107–8
Profitability, 6, 26, 28–30, 153, 166
Program management, 32–40
Property
 inspection, 49, 51
 location, 6
 salability, 52, 53, 147
Prospecting, xviii, 12, 13, 16–22, 58
 circle, 70, 127–28
 Joan's, 158
 kinds of calls, 18
 methods/scripts, 44
 model plan, 87
 plan, 4
 proactive, 124
 reactive, 73, 124
 results, 22, 242
 starting, 21–22
 yours, 16–17, 164
 week two, 90–91
Prospects, best source of, 16
Purchase and sale agreements, xv, 89, 104, 121

Q

Qualifying buyers, 43, 47, 52, 54, 121, 148
 appointment log, 54–56
 evaluating customer's potential, 56, 57
 potential, 149
 prospecting, 58
Qualifying questions, 48
Qualifying sellers, 43, 47, 48
 appointments, 146
 beginning process, 49, 50
 gathering information, 49, 51
 professionalism and, 48–49
Qualifying skills, development of, 47–48
Questioning, 47–48
 asking right, 45
 to get order, 134, 138

R

Rainmakers, 10
Reactive activities, 60, 73, 158, 164

Real estate
 nature of, 92
 technical aspects of, xiv, xv
Reality, 35
REALTOR®, 51, 90, 138
REALTOR® Magazine, 129
Referral fees, 33
Referrals, 16
Relationship marketing, 4–5, 126–27
 learning, 34
 systemization trend and, 19
 technology trends and, 19–20
 trend, 18
Relationship skills, 46
Revson, Charles, 52
Road map, xviii

S

Salability, 52, 53, 147
Sales
 activities, xiv, 25, 26
 importance of, xiii–xiv
Sales calls, xix, 104, 128
 crafting, 125–26
 script, 134, 135–37
Sales calls, 104
Sales calls, xix
Sales communication, 48
Sales script, 70, 131
Sales skills, xv, xvi, xix, 87
 critical, 43–44, 134–35
 listening and, 45
 practice, 43
Schedule, prototype, 15
Segment markets, 123–24
Self-efficacy, 106, 107–8
Self-management, 22, 31–32
Self-promotion, 16
Shadowing, 41
Showing/presenting, xviii
 movie, 108
Skill mastery, xvi
Social conversations, 48
Start-up plan, xii, xiv. *See also*
 Business start–up plan
 training and, 7
Student accountability, 7
Success
 agreement, 41, 42
 habits, xix

rate, for-sale-by-owner, 130
 stories, xii
Systematization trend, 5, 18–19, 104

T

Target market, 20, 123–24, 129
Teaming, 10
Technology trends, 5–6, 19–20
30 Days to Dollars, 43
 activity, 163
 best sources of business, 124
 Joan's
 first week, 72, 154
 fourth week, 120, 157
 prospecting, 158
 second week, 155
 third week, 103, 156
 lead sources, 128
 week two, 78, 88
 week four, 110
Tice, Lou, 40, 106
Tie down, 135, 141, 142
Time management, 56, 89–90
Training
 action focus, 4
 coaching and, 9–10
 interview and, 7–8
 trends in, 6–8
Training program, xiv–xvi, xix
 content and instruction methods, 7
 goal support in, xvi
 plans to avoid, xvii
Transactions completed, 90–91
Trends, 1

V

Value-added services, 54, 56, 58

W

Warm calling, 17
Web page, 6
Weekly activity plan, xix, 43, 61
 Joan's, 63, 160
 week one, 59–75
 week two, 78, 90
 week three, 94–102
 week four, 110
 yours, 62, 79, 95, 111
Weekly assignments, objectives, 25, 40
www.isucceed.com, 8